20 MYTHS

about Religion and
Politics in America

20 MYTHS

about Religion and
Politics in America

Ryan P. Burge

FORTRESS PRESS
Minneapolis

20 MYTHS ABOUT RELIGION AND POLITICS IN AMERICA

Cover design and illustration: Kris Miller

Print ISBN: 978-1-5064-8201-9
Ebook ISBN: 978-1-5064-8202-6

To the members (past and present) of
First Baptist Church of Mount Vernon, Illinois.
You took a chance on a twenty-four-year-old
kid and haven't gotten rid of me yet.

Contents

Preface

IN THE YEAR 2020, I CREATED A TOTAL OF 1,429 graphs. Almost all of them were about religion and politics. Trying to understand how these two facets of American society interact and intersect has been my professional focus over the past decade. It consumes a significant portion of my thoughts. I would be embarrassed to admit how many times I have jumped out of bed right before I fell asleep because an idea for a graph came to mind.

I wasn't always like this. For the first part of my academic career, I did what other scholars do: I wrote articles for peer-reviewed academic journals that only a handful of people read. I thought I needed to do that to secure my dream job as a college professor.

But a few years ago, I realized that writing for other academics was not bringing me joy, and I honestly wasn't that good at it. So I decided to change course a bit. I spent about two years becoming acquainted with some new tools to analyze and visualize data, and then I started regularly tweeting out graphs. Most of them don't get a lot of attention, but every once in a while, one will go viral and get hundreds of retweets and millions of views.

Slowly and steadily, I began to build a reputation as the religion-and-politics data guy. Members of the media started to reach out, asking questions about the graphs I posted and inquiring if there was data available to help them write their stories. As a result, my name has appeared in almost every major news outlet in the United States. That's been a real thrill for a kid who grew up in a small town in rural Illinois and certainly wasn't educated at the most prestigious universities.

But beyond the media coverage, other users of Twitter started tagging me when they saw something about politics and religion that they wondered about. Was it true? They were basically asking me to fact-check random strangers on the internet. It is kind of awkward to tell people through the internet that they are wrong. But I must admit it was nice to know that people began to see my work as authoritative.

So in the course of making thousands of graphs and composing hundreds of tweets, I started compiling a list of some of the common things that people write online that I know are false because I have the data to back it up. That's where the idea for this book came from. Instead of trying to describe why people's perceptions of religion and politics were wrong in 280 characters, I wanted to give each of these myths deeper treatment.

I love the fact that the subjects I study are of such great interest to the average American. I don't have to try to convince people that the work I do is valid and important. Yes, the downside is that lots of people have opinions about my field without any empirical evidence to back them up. But helping people to understand the world more accurately is where I find my bliss.

Beyond upsetting your thinking about the world around you, I hope my work will motivate you to seek out more answers to the questions underlying the myths I write about here and other incredibly important questions. There are plenty more myths that need to be busted in American politics and religion.

Introduction

The Facts Are In

WE CAN'T EVEN AGREE ON THE FACTS ANYMORE.
I was doing what I knew was a mistake. I got into an argument with someone on social media. They were making a point using statistical evidence that I knew to be false. So I did what I always do in situations like this: I made a graph. I sent that graph to him with a note that simply said, "I think that data you are relying on is faulty, and I have more confidence in these results that I'm illustrating here." The reply I got a few minutes later was direct and demoralizing: "I don't believe your data."

Trying to be data-driven, neutral, and objective is my entire career, my life's purpose, something I'd like to think that I am pretty good at. But no matter how much data, how many graphs, how much evidence I muster, this guy will never believe me. And he's not alone.

A growing segment of the population is completely unwilling to even entertain facts that may contradict the way that they think about politics, culture, and society. Huge swaths of the public seem to express no desire to rethink their worldview. I like to believe that American discourse used to be focused on high-minded ideas like freedom, morality, and the role of government in the lives of its citizens. Debates about the purpose of life, what is true, and what constitutes a good life are worth having, because they focus on what we value, how our life experiences shape our worldview, and what we hope and fear for the future.

The ancient Greeks believed that to bring your best argument to a debate was to give a gift to your opponent. It was understood as a means to help your opponent understand another perspective and to give your opponent the opportunity to rethink their own view of the world. Now, verbal exchanges are just about finding the wittiest comeback. We have strayed far from that Grecian model of public discourse. We can't even agree on what is empirically true. The line in our heads that separates what actually exists from creations of partisan media is unnervingly blurry these days.

THE BIG LIES

For instance: over half of Americans believe that the Earth's warming is not due to human activity. Overwhelming amounts of evidence from scientists of all political and academic backgrounds demonstrate that human beings have driven the climate crisis. Those who fail to believe in climate change are denying the work of tens of thousands of dedicated researchers across the globe who have arrived at the same conclusion.[1]

The share of Americans who believe that it is important for parents to vaccinate their children dropped ten percentage points between 2001 and 2015. Less than half of Americans could say with certainty that there is no causal link between vaccines and autism, despite the fact that there is zero scientific evidence that ties these two things together.[2]

Nearly half of Republicans today believe that President Joe Biden won the 2020 election through voter fraud and deception that happened on a multistate scale and involved hundreds of thousands of fraudulent ballots. This is in spite of the fact that none of the individuals amplifying these lies, when asked to describe their evidence under oath in a court of law, were willing to repeat these baseless conspiracies under penalty of perjury.[3]

It's not an exaggeration to say that when verifiable facts are in dispute, we are at a moment of crisis. If we think about the structure of political discourse, facts are the foundation. If we cannot agree on the foundation, there can be no meaningful debate. The Founders of the United States knew that spirited debate followed by painful compromise was the only way their system of democracy could work. But that's not how political discourse works now. The current level of political discourse in the United States could best be described as both sides rolling around in a mud pit, trying to get the other side dirtier than they are.

Observing the devolution of American debate over the past two decades has been especially jarring for me. I grew up in a conservative evangelical Southern Baptist church that was led by pastors who emphasized to me over and over again that there are objective Truths in this world. I can't tell you how many sermons I heard about the boogeyman of moral relativism. The phrase "all Truth is God's Truth" has been deeply embedded into my subconscious.

The same men and women who taught me those lessons in Sunday school and on church camping trips now try to tell anyone who follows them on social media to ignore the evidence from the scientific community, or courts of law, and instead to believe in random videos they find on YouTube or an article that was copied and pasted on social media with zero attribution or fact-checking.

I can't even begin to catalog the number of hours I spent as a child and teenager learning how to use the work of biologists, archeologists, and historians to defend the claim that the Bible is absolutely true. But when scientists working in those same fields tell us that burning fossil fuels leads to the rising sea levels, or that voter fraud is incredibly rare and hardly ever impacts the outcome of an election, their work, too many people assert, must be ignored, criticized, or at least overlooked.

THE SMALLER LIES

While high profile conspiracy theories take up a lot of bandwidth on social media and cable news networks, right below those are a menagerie of less outlandish but no less insidious lies about the way American society actually works. These haven't been pushed by hucksters trying to get more views on their videos or more shares for their content. Instead, these are suppositions about the world that people just naturally assume are true because they have never seen any real evidence to the contrary. These nuggets are considered by pastors, denominational leaders, and even people in the pews as true unless proven false. These myths, I'll call them, are worth really considering, because they form the foundation of our worldviews. Imagine a builder was tasked with constructing a new bridge made entirely of bricks. If he got lazy and decided not to carefully inspect all the bricks that would form the base of the bridge, eventually those faulty materials would lead to a catastrophic collapse. Similarly, we can expect collapse when our worldviews are too often built on a series of small, untested assumptions about the way things work.

You might ask, "How can having an inaccurate view of things like religion and politics have any real impact on society?" Let me give you an example of that. Some of my favorite types of survey questions ask respondents to describe how they view members of the other political party. These surveys provide an important window into just how unmoored perception can be from reality.

In a poll conducted in March 2015, two political scientists asked Republicans to estimate what share of the Democratic party are atheists or agnostics.[4] The average guess was 36 percent, but the reality is that only 9 percent of Democrats say they are atheists or agnostics. Republican respondents also believe that 38 percent of Democrats are lesbian, gay, or bisexual. In reality, just 6 percent say they are.

But this misperception cuts both ways. In the same poll, Democrats said they believed that 44 percent of Republicans were 65 or older. In reality, just 21 percent are. Additionally, Democrats believed that nearly half of Republicans made $250,000 a year or more. In reality just 2 percent of GOP members do.

While poll results like these are great for clickbait articles with titles like "Look how wrong Democrats are about Republicans," there is something much more dangerous going on just below that headline. The takeaway for me is this: Americans don't have a firm grasp of what the opposition actually looks like, and in the absence of actual data, they usually assume the worst about those on the other side of the aisle. In international relations there is a concept called the mirror image hypothesis, which contends that countries perceive the actions of other nations in terms of their own biases and cultural norms. Often, this approach leads to perceiving the other nation's behavior in the most nefarious terms, when the real motivation for that country's behavior is much more innocuous. Conflict, not compromise, is inevitable if one side always seeks to believe the worst about the other side.

In general, when there's a data vacuum, human beings tend to fill it not just with incorrect information but often with assumptions that are comically wrong. For those who advocate for the mirror image hypothesis, the best evidence of its potential consequences is the Cold War. The United States and the USSR spent hundreds of billions of dollars to develop weapons and defense systems in response to the actions of the other nation. Each side believed that the other was stockpiling weapons in anticipation of a nuclear war, something that thankfully never came to pass. Instead, when the Soviet Bloc finally collapsed due to economic and cultural pressure, Americans began to realize that the average Russian wasn't hell-bent on the destruction of the United States. Despite this realization, the arms race went on—with the Russians buying more weapons because the Americans were increasing their stockpile, and vice versa. Like those Cold War adversaries, political partisanship assumes the worst about the other end of the political spectrum when, in reality, Democrats and Republicans agree on a vast number of things. Yet fomenting conflict and painting the other side as extremists have become commonplace.

OVERCOMING THE LIES

So what's the antidote to this morass in which we find ourselves? It begins when people from all political persuasions start to embrace a worldview that is less partisan and more empirical.

To perceive the world in an empirical way is, in my estimation, a superpower. It means that emotion plays no role in how I receive and incorporate facts into my understanding of how society works. To be empirical is to rid myself of ideological, theological, and cultural bias and instead ruthlessly to seek out what is verifiably true in this world. If anything can unite a country that seems to be becoming more politically, economically, and religiously polarized every day, it's the embracing of an empirical worldview. It may be the only thing we can ever agree on in the future.

If the coronavirus pandemic taught me anything, it was that most Americans are not well equipped to think empirically about the world around them. The number of people who got on planes because they wanted to take a vacation was a testament to the fact that lots of people did not take seriously the empirical data concerning the contagiousness and lethality of COVID-19. But the fact that huge swaths of Americans refused to put their children back in school until every student was vaccinated is a testament to people relying on fear, not the science, to guide their decision-making.

I'm clearly engaging in wishful thinking to hope Americans, or anyone, will adopt an empirical worldview. I readily admit that—on a regular basis, I struggle with thinking empirically, and it's my life's work. But just because it's impossible to be completely empirical does not mean that seeking to be more and more empirical in our decision-making is not a laudable goal. Being empirical is uncomfortable, because it may challenge our suppositions of how the world works. It requires accepting evidence that challenges our worldview. But just because something is difficult doesn't mean it's not worthwhile. An empirical worldview gets us closer to what is true in the world than any other approach that we have at our disposal. And maybe my own bias as a pastor is showing, but seeking Truth is supposed to be the ultimate goal of any follower of Jesus Christ.

How do we begin to do that? Where do we start? We start with the facts.

Unfortunately, I am not an expert in climatology or virology. So if you want facts about climate change and vaccines, you are going to have to go somewhere else to find those. And even though I am a political scientist, I am not as well versed in voter fraud as many others in my field. They have reams of data at their fingertips and spend years honing arguments about how voter fraud is not a problem in this country. Listen to them—they are the authorities.

However, if you want information about religion and politics in the United States, I can help you, because I'm an expert in that field. The reason I can state that, by any objective measure, is that it is the truth. How did I acquire this expertise? In the same way that a plumber becomes a master at the craft or a violinist becomes the first chair in their symphony—through a dogged pursuit of becoming more knowledgeable in my field of study. I earned a doctoral degree in political science after six years of study and writing a dissertation that was focused on religion and political behavior in the United States. Since then I have published two dozen peer-reviewed articles on religion and politics in academic journals. I have written a book on the religiously unaffiliated in the United States and have contributed analysis about American religion and politics to some of the largest media outlets in the nation. I am regularly consulted by folks in the media, the church, and private industry about the current and future state of American religion.

It's not an exaggeration to say that I dig into the data almost every day of my life and have been doing so for the past five years. And I have the numbers to prove it. As previously mentioned, in 2020, I made a total of 1,429 graphs. That's about four graphs every single day of the year. And, yes, I did make a graph on Christmas. But I promise it was about how people observe holiday traditions!

I have cut every dataset a thousand different ways, looking for a new angle or a new story about American religion. It's the thing that I think about when I lie in bed at night or when I'm taking a shower. I have a running note on my phone where I gather ideas that hit me that I just have to explore.

There's something that happens when you work with data every day that I didn't fully understand until just a few years ago. Insights begin to materialize that lead to further analysis—and in my case, to an even deeper understanding of the religious and political landscape of the United States. After doing all that work, I've come to realize that the way that most people think about religion and politics is only loosely linked to any empirical reality. Instead, it's based on anecdotes, a quick scan of news headlines, or worse—just flat-out lies told by bad actors trying to push a religious or political agenda on a distracted public. That's incredibly caustic for the future of American politics and religion, because facts are the building blocks of not just debate but all aspects of a civilized society.

So I want to help you see what I see in the data. Some of it will upset you, some of it will surprise you, and hopefully some of it will change you. Altering our understanding of the world based on new information is not a sign of weakness but great intellectual strength. Can you imagine if we all had the same viewpoints that we held when we were eighteen? One of the most powerful images I've seen in the last few years was a man standing at a protest holding a small sign that said, "I'm sorry I'm late. I had a lot to learn." What a tremendous display of humility and openness.

I am reminded of the famous quote by James Baldwin: "Not everything that is faced can be changed; but nothing can be changed until it is faced."[5] If large swaths of the American public go through life with a fundamentally flawed understanding of the world around them and a misperception of where they fit into the larger fabric of society, they are never really facing the problems facing us. They are making decisions on whom to vote for on election day based only on caricatures of what our country really looks like. An educated electorate with a nuanced understanding of politics and government is insulated against the political rhetoric of politicians seeking office. The use of buzzwords and cherry-picked statistics does not change their minds. An engaged citizenry is immune to pandering, because citizens seek to elect people who have a clear vision for the future and can articulate how to implement policies that get closer to that ideal. I am reminded of the single sentence etched onto the grave of the famous philosopher John Locke: "I know there is truth opposite to falsehood that it may be found if people will & is worth the seeking." The Truth is undoubtedly worth seeking, and I hope this book helps many on that journey.

What follows are twenty short chapters, each of which focuses on myths I often hear discussed by casual observers of religion and politics. Half of the myths are about American religion, while the other half are focused on how religion interacts with politics in the United States. Each myth is just a bit over two thousand words and contains several graphs to illustrate my point. My aim is to make these myths accessible to the average reader. The statistics here are basic. In almost all cases, I am doing nothing more than counting things or calculating averages. (You can learn a lot about the world through some basic math.)

Because of space limitations, I cannot explore all the literature for each myth in great depth. But if a myth interests you, check out the key resources I have listed at the end of each myth to help you learn more about that topic. They provide a good starting point for a deeper journey into understanding the nuances of religion and politics.

Evangelicalism is in decline

EVERY FEW YEARS, A NATIONAL MEDIA OUTLET publishes a story about the inevitable decline of American religion. It all began with that famous *Time* magazine cover from April 1966. Three words in a bolded red font stood against a solid black background, "Is God Dead?" Of course, the editors were borrowing this idea from the famous German philosopher Friedrich Nietzsche, who wrote, "God is dead. God remains dead. And we have killed him." Nietzsche was making a point that the era of the Enlightenment and its push for scientific reasoning had eliminated a need for God, but most Americans did not know the full context of the quote. They just saw the magazine cover at the supermarket checkout stand, and many of them got angry. A retrospective on the piece noted that *Time* magazine received 3,241 letters from readers upon its publication. One of those letters stated, "Your ugly cover is a blasphemous outrage."⁶ Significant portions of the United States were devoutly religious in the 1960s, and to say that God was dead was an affront to their entire worldview.

Discussion surrounding the supposed death of religion, including evangelical Christianity in the United States, has only picked up steam since then. There seems to be a never-ending drumbeat of stories declaring the end of American religion.

The Atlantic ran a piece titled "Three Decades Ago, America Lost Its Religion. Why?,"[7] and just a few months later the *Week* published an article with the headline "The Coming End of Christian America."[8] That the country is becoming less religious as each day passes seems to be the highest-profile story in American religious demography. The American church is on a death spiral and will look like Western Europe's in the next few decades.

True, the story is not entirely manufactured or without some empirical merit. Ample evidence from a variety of data sources points to a continuing rise of the so-called nones in American society. The Pew Research Center noted that the nones were 16 percent of the US population in 2007, 23 percent in 2014, and 26 percent in 2019. I wrote a book about the topic myself, noting that the share of Americans with no religious affiliation may be as high as 30 percent, a finding I reached using a survey methodology different from Pew's.[9] No matter how the numbers are crunched, though, we can say that those without a religious affiliation are a larger share of America than ever before. Still, we need to keep in mind that the nones increasing doesn't necessarily mean all religious traditions are on the decline.

I do not blame the American public for believing that religion is in its twilight in our society. However, I think most people arrive at that conclusion by extrapolating a bit too much from the headlines they glance at as they scroll through the titles of books on Amazon, a news app, or their social media feed. They see, for instance, *The End of White Christian America*, a tremendous book written by Robert P. Jones, the CEO of the Public Religion Research Institute.[10] Or they notice Pew headlining its most recent report "In U.S., Decline of Christianity Continues at Rapid Pace."[11] No matter the source, they conclude that Christianity, writ large, is on its deathbed.

What they miss is that both Jones and the team at Pew lay out a very nuanced and careful story that highlights how certain types of American religion, not all of Christianity, are in decline. The story of what is happening to American Christianity is much more complicated than any headline could ever really capture and, in my opinion, is even more interesting. The real story of American Christianity is that those who are intensely religious have not changed in any meaningful way in the past fifty years.

Dozens of stories written in the past few years claim the opposite. Headlines like "The Deepening Crisis in Evangelical Christianity" [12] and "Blame Evangelicals for the Decline in Christian Faith"[13] reinforce a narrative that evangelicalism has become poisonous to the average American and pews are emptier now than ever before. Observers point to this demise especially in those churches that are more conservative on theological and political matters.

Yet when I read those stories and look at the data, I just can't help but think that for many critics of evangelicalism, the decline of the movement is nothing more than wishful thinking. No matter which dataset I use or how I define "evangelical," I am unable to find strong and consistent evidence that evangelicals are a less significant part of the population today than they were forty years ago.

The General Social Survey (GSS) has been asking questions about religious affiliation since 1972 and is considered the only authoritative source for tracking the composition of American religion over a long time horizon. Thus, it makes sense to start there when trying to understand what has happened to evangelicals over the past forty years.

When the trend line for evangelicals is illustrated in the GSS, an interesting interpretation puzzle emerges. The left plot in

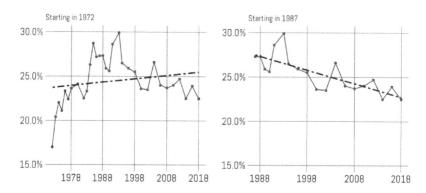

Figure 1.1. Share of Americans Who Are Evangelical by Tradition—Two Different Starting Points

Data from the General Social Survey, a project of the independent research organization NORC at the University of Chicago, with principal funding from the National Science Foundation, https://gss.norc.org/Get-The-Data

figure 1.1 displays the data all the way back to the inception of the survey—1972. The right plot truncates that time horizon to the peak of American evangelicalism, which occurred in the late 1980s and early 1990s. As the dashed line indicates in the plot on the left, the trend for American evangelicals in the United States is a slightly upward one over forty-six years. They were just under 24 percent of the population in the early 1970s and rose to just over 25 percent in 2018.

Despite this slightly upward trend, many people focus on what has happened to evangelicals since their peak around 1993, shown by the trend line in the right panel. If we begin our analysis in 1987, the slope of the line is clearly negative. In statistical terms, nearly 28 percent of Americans were evangelical in 1987 and that has dropped about five percentage points in the past thirty years.

But that second narrative ignores two key pieces of relevant evidence. The first is that evangelicals today are the same percentage of the US population in 2018 that they were in 1982—a fact that does not support the "evangelicals are dying" hypothesis. The other is that the decline of evangelicalism has basically stopped since 2000. In that year, evangelicals were 23.6 percent of the sample. In 2018, they were 22.5 percent. That drop of one percentage point is not statistically significant, nor is it substantively noteworthy, because the share of evangelicals has see-sawed between 23 and 24 percent in the past several years.

Instead of claiming a decline in evangelicalism, the more objective perspective is that the period from the late 1980s through the late 1990s was an aberration in the history of American religion. Because of a confluence of a number of religious, cultural, and political shifts, evangelicalism saw a significant but relatively short-lived burst in popularity. The more honest reading of the data is that evangelicals constitute just slightly less than a quarter of Americans in an average year, and there is little reason to think that this will substantially shift in the next decade.

However, there's another way to measure the size of evangelicalism over time—self-identification. The prior analysis did not rely on a survey respondent saying they were an evangelical. Instead, they told the survey administrator what denomination the church they attended belongs to, and social scientists sorted them into the evangelical camp based on just that information. However, many surveys have begun to include an additional question about religious identification: "Do you consider yourself to be a born-again or evangelical Christian, or not?" The person hearing the question determines their religious attachment.

To that end, since 1988 the GSS has been asking this question, "Would you say you have been 'born-again' or have had a 'born-again' experience—that is, a turning point in your life when you committed yourself to Christ?" The results of those responses are shown in figure 1.2 and show a slow upward trajectory in the past three decades. About 37 percent of Americans said in 1988 that they had had a born-again experience, but by 2004 that had dropped by about three percentage points. From that point forward there has been a slow and steady climb in the share of Americans who say they have had a born-again experience. The born-again portion of the sample jumped by four percentage points between 2004 and 2010 and then has increased just about four percentage points again from 2010 to 2018. In the most recent data available, the share of Americans who say they have had a born-again experience is 41 percent. There's definitely no sign of evangelical decline from that angle.

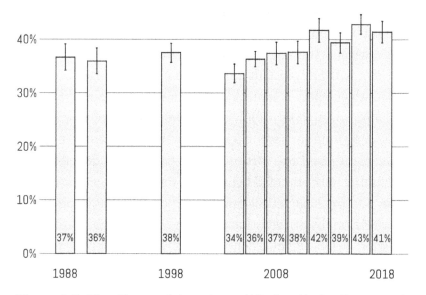

Figure 1.2. The Share of Americans Who've Had a Born-Again Experience

Data from the General Social Survey, a project of the independent research organization NORC at the University of Chicago, with principal funding from the National Science Foundation, https://gss.norc.org/Get-The-Data

However, that question is not perfect for measuring the current size of the evangelical population in the United States for two reasons. One is based on the wording of the question: "Have you *ever* had a born-again experience?" Someone could have gone forward during an altar call at a high school church camp but since become an avowed atheist. They would still answer that question affirmatively, although they clearly aren't an evangelical today. The other issue is that the question doesn't specifically mention the term "evangelical," although it does clearly refer to a conversion experience that is closely linked to the evangelical experience. Still, some survey respondents may not make the connection between being born-again and embracing an evangelical identity on their own.

Both using religious denomination to classify evangelicals and asking about a born-gain experience obviously are problematic. However, there's a more straightforward way to assess evangelicalism in the public: just ask people directly if they identify as an evangelical Christian. If the term "evangelical" has become somewhat radioactive for a wide swath of the American population and has led to the decline of evangelicalism, using it clearly in a survey question would reveal that aversion. Indeed, respondents' reluctance to identify themselves as evangelical might be expected in our current climate. As the linkage between the Republican Party and evangelical Christianity has grown closer over the past few years, the connection may have turned off a few more politically moderate Protestant Christians. Additionally, the election and widespread support of Donald Trump by white evangelicals during his time in the White House could have made the term more caustic in the eyes of the American public. But when people are asked directly if they are evangelicals, we see no evidence of the "evangelicals are in decline" hypothesis.

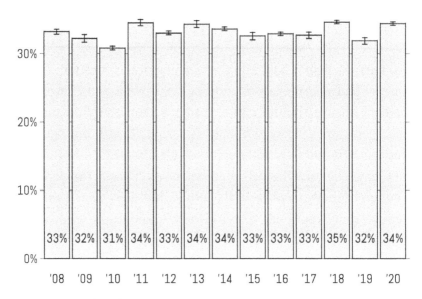

Figure 1.3. The Share of Population That Identifies as Born-Again/ Evangelical

Data from Cooperative Election Study. Stephen Ansolabehere, Brian F. Schaffner, and Sam Luks, Cambridge, MA: Harvard University, http://cces.gov.harvard.edu

The Cooperative Election Study (CES) has been asking the evangelical self-identification question in every survey it has administered since 2008, and the results are remarkably consistent, as can be seen in figure 1.3. In 2008, exactly one-third of respondents said they that were born-again or evangelical. That number has held steady in nearly every wave of their study. That figure has gone as high as 34.6 percent and as low as 30.8 percent, but the overall average is 33.1 percent, and most years' findings deviate from that average by less than one percentage point. What makes this finding even more noteworthy is how large the sample size is for the CES. The smallest wave is 14,000 respondents, and the largest is nearly 65,000. When numbers in a survey get that large, conclusions come into sharper focus: the term "evangelical" was no more or less poisonous after three years of a Trump presidency than it was the year Barack Obama won the White House.

CONCLUSIONS

If evangelicalism is demarcated by religious tradition, the evidence clearly indicates that evangelicals are the same share of the population today that they were during Ronald Reagan's first term. I cannot imagine that most Americans would assume that evangelicals were on the ropes in 1982, and if that's true then they could not in good conscience make this claim about evangelicals in 2022. They have clearly declined from their peak in 1993, but that decline almost entirely abated by 2000. From that point forward, the story is one of relative stability and durability.

For Further Reading

Fitzgerald, Frances. *The Evangelicals: The Struggle to Shape America*. New York: Simon and Schuster, 2017.

> Fitzgerald's book on evangelicals has quickly become one of the most authoritative works on the spiritual movement in the United States. The real value in this work is Fitzgerald's neutral approach to the topic. At times, her writing seems sympathetic to the cause of evangelical Christianity, while in other sections she seems much more critical of the group.

Kidd, Thomas. *Who Is an Evangelical?: The History of a Movement in Crisis*. New Haven, CT: Yale University Press, 2019.

> Thomas Kidd is one of the widely read evangelical historians in the United States, and this book on evangelicals is worth a read. Using his tremendous historical prowess, Kidd

describes in clear prose the history of the movement in the United States. Kidd ends his volume by arguing that evangelicals are not naturally inclined to be overly partisan but were mobilized to vote for the Republicans by several well-respected evangelical organizations.

Noll, Mark A., David W. Bebbington, and George M. Marsden. *Evangelicals: Who They Have Been, Are Now, and Could Be.* Grand Rapids, MI: Wm. B. Eerdmans Publishing, 2019.

This edited volume contains chapters from some of the best-known evangelical scholars from around the world. The content of this book touches on topics such as the theological underpinnings of evangelical thought as well as a section focused on evangelicals' affinity for Donald Trump.

Donald Trump wasn't the choice of religiously devout Republicans

I AM ALWAYS INTERESTED IN THE SOURCE OF MISPER-
ceptions about Donald Trump's support. The news and analysis
surrounding his strong showing in the polls during the run-up to
the early primaries in 2016 makes clear that the media was looking for a narrative. Many in the pundit class were scrambling for
an outside-the-box explanation for an unconventional candidate
like Donald Trump doing so well in states where the Republican
base consisted largely of conservative Catholics and evangelicals.
In the absence of any solid data source, which the general public
rarely has access to, the public grab onto storylines that are often
hastily constructed and prove to be faulty when subjected to more
rigorous analysis.

If we think back to what was happening in American politics
in 2015 and early 2016, we recall the beginnings of a significant
shift in the direction of the Republican party. The prior two presidential candidates to emerge from crowded Republican primary
fields (John McCain in 2008 and Mitt Romney in 2012) could best
be described as mainstream, moderate, and consensus-building.
John McCain made his name in the national political scene by
breaking from Republican orthodoxy on a number of issues, such
as campaign finance reform and climate change. Mitt Romney
was quite proud of his term as governor of the deeply blue state of

Massachusetts, which instituted a government-run health insurance program for its residents under his leadership.

Thus, the general thinking was that the Republican party would continue to nominate relatively moderate candidates to national office. Because religious voters make up a large share of the GOP, it was fair to assume that they were the ones propelling moderate candidates to the highest ranks of the Republican establishment. Thus, it only made sense that someone like Ted Cruz or Marco Rubio, both fairly conservative but with religious bona fides, would emerge from a brutal Republican primary as the victor.

But that narrative fell apart very quickly as the primary voters in early-voting states went to the polls. Donald Trump began to pull away from the pack and was enjoying substantial leads in the polling over Ted Cruz, Marco Rubio, John Kasich, and the rest of the GOP field in a number of key states.[14] After suffering a small defeat to Ted Cruz in the Iowa caucuses, Trump went on a streak of victories, winning New Hampshire, South Carolina, and Nevada by double-digit margins. By early March, the race was all but over.

Thus, political analysts were in a bit of a bind. The results on election day don't lie. Trump was racking up clear victories from very early on in the race. So where was his support coming from? If it wasn't conservative Christians backing his candidacy, who was his base? A narrative began to emerge in those early days of Iowa and New Hampshire that Donald Trump was winning these races not because of strong support from evangelicals who were attending worship services frequently. Instead, the story became that Trump was the darling of Republicans who didn't really go to church—that those secular voters were propelling him to victory.

The primary driver of that narrative was Timothy Carney. In his book *Alienated America*, Carney uses data from the Voter Study

Group and finds that among all Republican primary voters, Trump won majorities of those who seldom or never attended church but received votes from only a third of those who attended church more than once a week.[15]

But that is a very specific way to read the data that seems to downplay some important realities about what the Republican electorate looked like in early 2016. Using the same dataset that Carney does and restricting the sample to (1) individuals who identified as Republicans and (2) also indicated they voted in the Republican primary, a much more nuanced picture emerges, as can be seen in figure 2.1.

Carney is absolutely correct in saying that Republican primary voters who never went to church were the most enthusiastic for Donald Trump, as he won two-thirds of this slice of the electorate. But how big is that slice? It was 20 percent of all Republican primary voters back in 2016. Trump, however, still does remarkably well at all other levels of church attendance. He bested Ted Cruz by 34 points among those who seldom attend church, and had a twenty-six-point advantage among yearly attenders. Among those who reported monthly attendance he also dominated, taking about three in five voters in a field of at least four viable candidates. While the supposed darling of the religious establishment, Ted Cruz, could muster only 20 percent. Even among more religiously devout GOP primary voters, where Carney claims we see things begin to shift, however, Trump's lead continues to hold. Among those who reported attending church once a week, Trump got half of the primary vote, while Cruz got about 30 percent. Only among those who attended services more than once a week does Trump fall behind. Cruz earned 39 percent of this group, compared to 31 percent for Trump.

But before we make some sweeping claim about how Trump did not do well with committed Christians, there are several things to keep in mind. Even among the most devout Republicans,

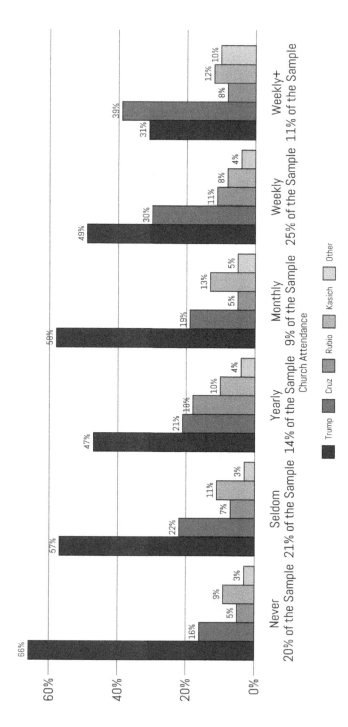

Figure 2.1. Candidate Choice among Republican Voters in 2016

Data from the VOTER (Views of the Electorate Research Survey), administered by the Democracy Fund's Voter Study Group. Los Angeles: University of California. https://www.voterstudygroup.org/data

Trump got nearly a third of primary votes. And Ted Cruz never reached that level of support among Republicans at any other attendance level. In other words, even in Trump's worst church attendance category, he did better than Ted Cruz did among voters at any other level of church attendance.

The other thing to consider is the size of each of these attendance buckets. Just 11 percent of all voters in the Republican primary attended church more than once per week, while 25 percent of them attended weekly. If those two attendance categories were combined into a single attendance category of "weekly or more," Trump received 44 percent of the vote, and Cruz garnered 32 percent. Thus, only a very narrow reading of the data supports the claim that Trump's base of support was among Republicans who never or rarely went to church when he still bested Ted Cruz among the most religiously devout Republican primary voters.

But why would the myth that Donald Trump's lack of support among religiously devout Republicans become so deeply ingrained in the public's understanding about religion and politics? I think the best explanation is that some commentators want to believe that Donald Trump is evidence that the Republican Party has become less religious over time and thus that the religious voters in the GOP (who favored a candidate like Ted Cruz) are being overwhelmed by the non-religious members of the Republican electorate (who supported Donald Trump). If that were true, then Trump's victory in the primary was more about the rise of the non-religious among the ranks of the Republicans and not really a referendum on Trump's widespread support among religious Republicans. But that's a fairly easy theory to test.

If the real impetus for Trump's victory was the changing composition of the Republican electorate, we should see that

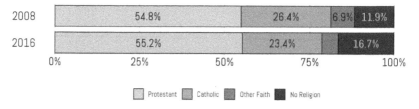

Figure 2.2. Religious Composition of the Republican Primary Electorate

Data from Cooperative Election Study. Stephen Ansolabehere, Brian F. Schaffner, and Sam Luks, Cambridge, MA: Harvard University, http://cces.gov.harvard.edu

the religious makeup of all Republicans who voted in the 2016 primaries looks a lot different from the group who voted for John McCain in the primary eight years earlier. The Cooperative Election Study provides the data to test that conclusion, which is visualized in figure 2.2.

In 2008, just about 55 percent of all Republican primary voters were Protestants. Another 26 percent were Catholics. Over seven in ten Republicans in 2008 were from a Christian tradition. In addition, about 7 percent were from other faith groups, including Latter-day Saints (LDS), Hindus, Muslims, Jews, and Buddhists. Finally, about 12 percent of the GOP primary base were those without a religious affiliation.

So how much did things shift eight years later? Very little. The same share of the Republican base was Protestant in 2016 compared to 2008—55 percent. The share of Catholics did decline by about three percentage points in eight years, however. Those of other faiths declined about two points as well. The share of the GOP that had no religious affiliation rose by just less than 5 percent in eight years. Thus, from this angle, there's little reason to believe that the nones played a significantly larger role in the nomination of Donald Trump in 2016 than they did in choosing John McCain as their party's nominee just eight years earlier.

CONCLUSIONS

One of the most revelatory things I learned in reading social science as a graduate student is the sheer number of cognitive biases each of us holds and how many of them we fall prey to without knowing it. An example is hindsight bias—our tendency to look on events from the past and perceive them in such a way that leads us to constantly say to ourselves, "We should have seen this coming." Often people do this at the end of a failed romantic relationship or after putting up with months or years of a poor work environment. We often see the warning signs in hindsight, when in actuality we could never have assumed that this is where things would end up. The result often makes us feel like we are inadequate and unable to make good decisions. The reality is that we are just too hard on ourselves.

Despite the fact that Donald Trump did end up winning both the Republican nomination and the presidency in 2016, there are many aspects of Trump's political performance that likely gives many of his supporters pause. He lost the popular vote in both 2016 and 2020. He was impeached twice, the second time for inciting an insurrection that led to loss of life on the grounds of the United States Capitol. Donald Trump was unable to win reelection, a rare occurrence for an incumbent president. And in the days after he left office, he publicly mused about the possibility of starting a new political party by drawing some of his strongest supporters from the GOP.

Many of the people who were trying to drive the narrative that the nonreligious were the key to Trump's primary victory are now engaging in hindsight bias, looking at other Republicans and saying, "we told you so" or "you should have seen how this was going to end." But their entire outlook on Trump's ascendancy seems to be predicated on a belief that Donald Trump is not who religious voters really wanted as their nominee. They want to believe that an insurgent coalition of secular Republicans catapulted Trump to the top of the pack. Trying to square Trump's personal moral failings with such rabid support by conservative evangelicals and Catholics.

I was born in the early 1980s and raised in a politically and theologically conservative Southern Baptist Church in the 1990s. That most salient political moment of my teenage years was the scandal related to President Bill Clinton's affair with Monica Lewinsky. That event happened when I was the most active in the youth group of my church, so I heard lots of discussion from both the pulpit and the pews about the incident. The one phrase that I distinctly remember being uttered by many trusted leaders in the church was "personal morality matters." Christians wanted a president who not only supported moral policies but also lived a life based on moral principles. Obviously, President Clinton had acted in an immoral way in his relations with the young intern, and he deserved to be impeached.

However, less than two decades later those same men and women who told me repeatedly that personal morality mattered threw their support behind a man who had been divorced twice, allegedly cheating on each wife, filed for bankruptcy multiple times, and uttered swear words during his stump speech to audiences of all ages. It makes complete sense that many observers of American politics would find it hard to believe that Donald Trump's strongest supporters were likely the same people who called for Clinton's ouster just two decades earlier. However, the data also indicates that white evangelicals had shifted their views significantly. The Public Religion Research Institute posed this question to white evangelicals: "Do you think an elected official who commits an immoral act in their personal life can still behave ethically and fulfill their duties in their public and professional life?" Thirty percent agreed that this elected official could fulfill their duties in 2011. It was 72 percent in 2016.[16] In essence, the simplest explanation is the best: religious conservatives changed their views to justify their preferred candidate.

For Further Reading

Carney, Tim P. *Alienated America: Why Some Places Thrive While Others Collapse.* New York: HarperCollins, 2019.

Tim Carney traveled all around the United States visiting rural and urban communities to write this interesting book about parts of America that are thriving in the twenty-first century while others are dying. While I don't agree with Carney's analysis of the survey data, his observations about how huge swaths of the United State are falling behind educationally, socially, and economically are spot on.

Fea, John. *Believe Me: The Evangelical Road to Donald Trump.* Grand Rapids, MI: Wm. B. Eerdmans Publishing, 2018.

John Fea is one of the most well-known public historians today who also identifies as an evangelical Christian. In this devastating book, Fea concludes that the election of Donald Trump was the culmination of decades of evangelicalism preaching a gospel based on fear and promising a return to a bygone era.

Posner, Sarah. *Unholy: How White Christian Nationalists Powered the Trump Presidency, and the Devastating Legacy They Left Behind.* New York: Random House, 2021.

Posner does a superb job of describing how evangelicals have always had a fraught relationship with racism in the United States. Her archival work is apparent in sections that detail how churches and pastors fought school integration every step of the way in many parts of the rural South. She also rightly notes how many of the nationalistic impulses of Christian conservatives have found a receptive audience among far-right groups in Europe.

MYTH 3

Most Americans have strong views about abortion—but are willing to change their minds about it

WHEN PEOPLE THINK ABOUT WHAT SCHOLARS OF American religion and politics study, I bet a lot of them think we spend a lot of our time on the topic of abortion. It may be the most religiously tinged policy debate in the United States. In actuality, very few social scientists build an entire research agenda around abortion. I try to avoid it as much as possible on social media, because it may be the most impassioned policy debate in the United States today. No matter how carefully I tread around abortion or what terminology I use, I quickly realize that to talk about abortion is to walk a tightrope over a pit of piranhas. One false word and you can quickly find yourself neck deep in water with some very hungry fish.

But that's not the only reason most scholars of religion and politics avoid the topic of abortion. The real reason is that it's just not that interesting from a data standpoint. Social scientists are human, and we know that when we write peer-reviewed articles, it's easier to get things published when we explore big swings in public opinion. And the data is fairly clear on this point: opinions about abortion have been stable for the past forty-five years.

Thus we have two different but deeply interrelated myths. The first is that the American public is highly polarized on abortion, with huge portions of the public consistently opposed to abortion and another significant portion favoring abortion access in most scenarios. The second myth, one that intuitively contradicts the first, is that public opinion on abortion is highly malleable. Consider all the time and money that has been spent on lobbying, literature, policy studies, social media posts, and protests outside state capitols and facilities where pregnancy and abortion counseling and services are provided over the past forty years.

Instead, what emerges from any analysis that tracks opinion about abortion over a long period is that the American public is surprisingly practical about women's rights and abortion restrictions. There have been some gradual shifts in how permissive the public is, but that's highly contextualized based on the reason a woman would seek out an abortion.

A good place to start a data inquiry is the most general question surrounding abortion: Would you support a woman having access to an abortion for any reason? That's conveyed in the top left graph in figure 3.1. In the 1970s, 44 percent of Americans who didn't go to church frequently supported a woman's right to choose. That's increased to 54 percent in the past four decades. For those who frequently attend services, support is lower overall. Just 18 percent of weekly churchgoers took a more permissive position in the 1970s. But data from the 2010s indicates that support for abortion on demand has actually gone up about five percentage points among weekly attenders.

However, when we dive into individuals' thinking about a woman's reasons for seeking an abortion, a much more nuanced portrait of Americans (religious and not) emerges. For instance, the public is still generally supportive of women having access to an abortion if there's a serious birth defect in the baby, but support has declined seven points for those who attend infrequently and eighteen points for those who are weekly attenders. Support

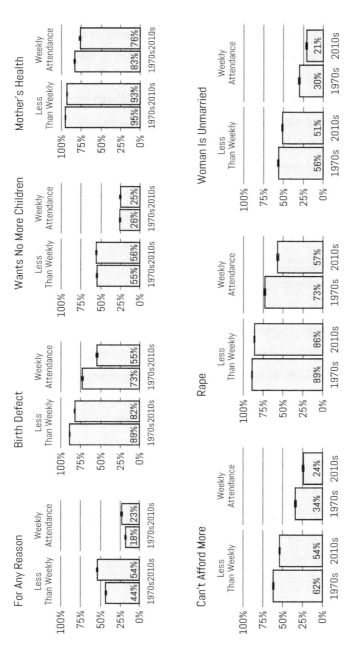

Figure 3.1. Support for Access to Abortion in Different Scenarios in the 1970s vs. 2010s

Data from the General Social Survey, a project of the independent research organization NORC at the University of Chicago, with principal funding from the National Science Foundation, https://gss.norc.org/Get-The-Data

for women having the option of seeking abortion when they don't want more children has also seen a similar decline. But in most cases the drop in non-churchgoers' support is similar to that of people who attend more frequently, although obviously the latter group is less permissive of abortion overall.

But in the aggregate, these shifts (especially in the less religious portion of the population) are small when considering a forty-year time span. Think about how much generational replacement has occurred during that time frame, with older, more conservative Americans dying off and being replaced by younger, more liberal ones. Yet in spite of that turnover, overall public opinion has shifted no more than ten percentage points in any of the seven scenarios. For comparison, in 1988 only 12 percent of Americans favored same-sex marriage. By 2018, 66 percent did. It's really hard to move the public's opinion on abortion.

But the lack of significant change in overall opinions is not the only misperception when it comes to abortion. The other myth that people seem to believe about abortion is that it is a highly polarized issue—that huge swaths of the American public are either completely in favor of access to abortion in all scenarios or completely opposed to abortion for any reason at any time. There are plenty of reasons to explain why people misperceive views on the issue. One of the primary factors that skew perception is media coverage of abortion. Just think about the type of people who are asked to go on cable news shows or podcasts and talk about abortion. Guests are almost always activists who have made a name for themselves by staking out extreme opinions. Moderates don't make for good television, and they typically don't show up with protest signs in front of abortion providers or join marches for a woman's right to choose. Extreme voices are often the loudest voices, and that's especially the case when it comes to abortion.

The Cooperative Election Study has been asking respondents their views on access to abortion in a variety of scenarios that help to paint a more nuanced portrait than just the pro-life/pro-choice divide. Those five questions are prefaced by asking, "Do you support or oppose the following policy?"

1. Always allow a woman to obtain an abortion as a matter of choice.
2. Ban abortion after the twentieth week of pregnancy.
3. Allow employers to decline coverage of abortion in insurance plans.
4. Prohibit the use of federal funds for abortion.
5. Make abortions illegal in all circumstances.

Responses to these five questions were scored. The pro-life answer was counted as zero, and the pro-choice option was counted as one. Combined, this scoring system created a scale ranging from zero (opposed to abortion in all five scenarios) to five (supportive of access to abortion). For instance, if an individual is opposed to abortion in all scenarios, but still does not want to make it completely illegal, they would score a one. The left panel in figure 3.2 is a fairly good approximation of how many Americans perceive the public's views about access to abortion. Many people believe huge portions of the public either score a zero or a five, and almost no one stands in the middle when it comes to abortion. However, the data paints a much different portrait of how Americans really think about abortion, as is clear in figure 3.2.

The panel on the right displays the actual distribution of scores on the abortion-access scale. The first impression that emerges is just how flat the distribution is. No score on the scale is much lower than 10 percent of the population, and no score is higher than 21 percent. Americans are truly all over the map in their thinking about access to abortion. It is clear, though, that the

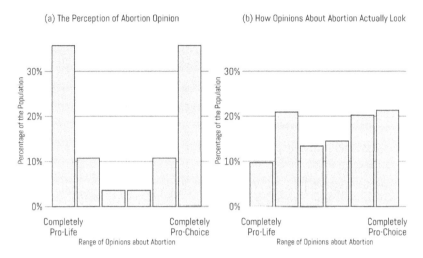

Figure 3.2. The Perception of Abortion Opinions vs. How Opinions about Abortion Actually Look

Data from Cooperative Election Study. Stephen Ansolabehere, Brian F. Schaffner, and Sam Luks, Cambridge, MA: Harvard University, http://cces.gov.harvard.edu

least popular position is for abortion to be completely illegal. Only about 10 percent of the public is located at that spot on the scale. However, the other end of the scale—support for access to abortion in all scenarios—occurs about twice as frequently.

To put some actual figures on this distribution: about 31 percent scored a zero or a one on the scale, while 41 percent of Americans scored a four or five. That leaves 28 percent of the sample in the middle of distribution. That's not what anyone would call a highly polarized electorate when it comes to abortion policy.

But what role does religion play in this? The perception that many people seem to have is that to be religious in the United States is to be strongly opposed to abortion, and that those who are less attached to a religious tradition are more permissive of a woman's right to end her pregnancy. To test that notion, I calculated across the church attendance spectrum the share of Americans that believe abortion should be completely illegal and the share that believes a woman should have access to an abortion for any reason. It's important to note that these two questions only tap into the extreme positions on each side of the abortion debate, because, as previously described, most people have a much more nuanced opinion.

It should come as no surprise that among those who never attend church services, support for access to abortion is robust, as is visualized in figure 3.3. Over three-quarters of never-attenders think a woman should be able to have an abortion if she wants one, and only 8 percent think that abortion should always be illegal. But as church attendance increases, support for access to abortion begins to drop. Among monthly attenders, about half

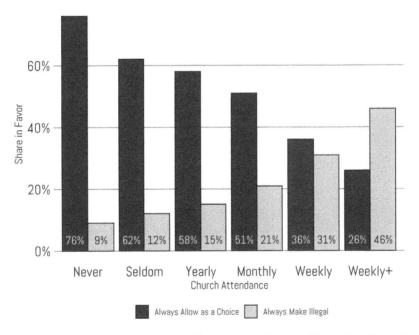

Figure 3.3. Support for Pro-Life/Pro-Choice Positions by Church Attendance

Data from Cooperative Election Study. Stephen Ansolabehere, Brian F. Schaffner, and Sam Luks, Cambridge, MA: Harvard University, http://cces.gov.harvard.edu

support access to abortion for any reason. However, that support is cut in half (to just 26 percent) among those who attend services more than once per week.

At the same, time there's clearly a positive relationship between frequency of church attendance and a desire to see abortion made completely illegal. However, the strength of that association is not as strong as many people perceive it to be. Consider this: a weekly churchgoer in the United States is more likely to support access to abortion without restriction than they are to favor making abortion always illegal. Only when we focus solely on those who attend church more than once a week do we see that the pro-life position clearly surpasses the pro-choice option.

But there are two important things to note about this category of highest church attendance. First, among respondents who attended a religious service multiple times a week, a majority still do not believe abortion should be made completely illegal in the United States. That's something worth repeating: even among the most religiously devout, support for an outright ban on abortion is mixed. Second, notice just how small a portion of the population this attendance category represents. Just 8 percent of Americans indicated they attend church with this frequency. For comparison, 30 percent of Americans say that they never attend religious services.

CONCLUSIONS

There are two clear takeaways from a careful analysis of public opinion surrounding abortion in the United States. The first is that the public's perception of abortion policy has been remarkably stable since the early 1970s. The share of Americans who identify as Christians has dropped by about twenty percentage points, yet our collective view of abortion has shifted little, especially among the non-religious.

The other finding that likely comes as a surprise to many readers is just how few Americans have a truly black-and-white view of abortion. Just about one in ten Americans say they are completely opposed to abortion, while only two in ten support access to abortion across the board. That leaves 70 percent of the public somewhere in between.

This interpretation comports well with research conducted by Tricia Bruce, a sociologist at Notre Dame University. She interviewed 217 subjects about abortion, asking probing questions about their views of abortion in a variety of scenarios and for many different reasons. What she found was that many respondents openly contradicted themselves during their interview, and when it was pointed out that they had contradictory opinions, the respondents readily recognized this tension and couldn't consistently explain how they arrived at their current view of abortion policy. Bruce's report notes that "mutually exclusive labels like 'pro-choice' and 'pro-life' fit Americans and the abortion issue imperfectly, at best."[17]

This is not the only time that I will analyze the opinions of Americans on abortion in this volume, but I do so with a great deal of trepidation. Most Americans seem to prefer sensible, moderate policy when it comes to abortion. When a politician is asked in a town hall how they feel about abortion, a response that is nuanced, sympathetic, and doesn't fit into a sound bite is unlikely to ignite a base of support. But that's really where most Americans stand on the issue of abortion.

For Further Reading

Bruce, Tricia C. *How Americans Understand Abortion: A Comprehensive Interview Study of Abortion Attitudes in the U.S.* South Bend, IN: University of Notre Dame, McGrath Institute for Church Life, 2020.

Bruce describes the nuanced opinions that exist among Americans around abortion. Pulling direct quotes from the interviews and weaving those through the report really drive home the fact that the vast majority of Americans don't have concrete positions and fully embrace the uncertainty of their views on the controversial topic.

Reagan, Leslie J. *When Abortion Was a Crime: Women, Medicine, and Law in the United States, 1867–1973*. Oakland, CA: University of California Press, 1997.

Most of us have never lived in the United States when abortion was not legal. However, for most of the history of our country, that was not the case. This wonderful book delves into the history of abortion in the hundred years before abortion was legalized in Roe v. Wade.

Ziegler, Mary. *Abortion and the Law in America: Roe v. Wade to the Present*. Cambridge, MA: Cambridge University Press, 2020.

If you are interested in a legal history of abortion in the United States, look no further than this valuable resource. This book points out how the debate over abortion extends to a number of areas of American life, including our views of the rights of children and our understanding of medical ethics.

Researchers are biased toward Christians

I WRITE ABOUT EVANGELICAL CHRISTIANS A LOT. It's almost impossible not to do that in the current religious and political climate in the United States. But inevitably when I post a graph on social media that is focused on the political behavior or vote choice of white evangelicals, someone in the comments says there's a media bias against other religious groups in the United States. Often I am accused of ignoring—being biased against— important segments of the American religious landscape such as Latter-day Saints, Buddhists, Hindus, or Wiccans, simply because I don't talk about them much. I'm becoming increasingly aware that people want to see analysis about their specific group. They want to know if their life experience is consistent with the data. But in many cases, the kind of analysis they are seeking is just not available.

I am always thinking about my blind spots in my research agenda. Am I focused too much on a specific religious group and not enough on another? That's a question that takes up an inordinate amount of my mental energy. For me, writing about Christians is easier because I grew up evangelical and I am now a pastor at an American Baptist Church. But I think the myth that the media and academia are obsessed with Christianity is not primarily rooted in any type of bias (either explicit or implicit) but instead in a statistical reality that most people never really consider.

Let me pull back the curtain just a bit on how all those charts and graphs come to be. Most researchers rely on survey data that is funded, fielded, and distributed by other organizations. Most of us have no other option than to use this data, and therefore we are at the mercy of decisions made by something else. Unfortunately, until just about a decade ago, very few religious groups had sufficient numbers in these surveys to study with any statistical accuracy. There's no "hard and fast" rule about the size of the group that is necessary to conduct statistical analysis, but having at least one hundred respondents is a good starting point. That means no analysis can be conducted on a group like Jews, unless there's one hundred of them. But if a more fine-grained analysis is desired, like Jewish women for instance, the total number of Jews in the sample would need to be about two hundred. So the reason journalists and academics didn't try to shine a light on female Latter-day Saints or young Buddhists is not that they didn't want to. They simply could not do it in an analytically rigorous way.

It's probably helpful to visualize just what I mean when I say that it's hard to study smaller religious groups on a survey. Figure 4.1 is a treemap, where each square represents the size of a religious group in the 2018 sample of the Cooperative Election Study. As can be quickly ascertained, three groups dominate American religion. Protestants are 38 percent of the population, nothing in particulars are 20 percent, and Catholics are 18 percent. Those three groups combined make up three-quarters of the entire American population. Thus, it's understandable why the lion's share of religious writing would focus on Christians in the United States, as they make up 56 percent of the entire country.

However, once you move past those three large religious groups, there's a significant gap before you move to the next three groups: atheists, agnostics, and the "something else" category,

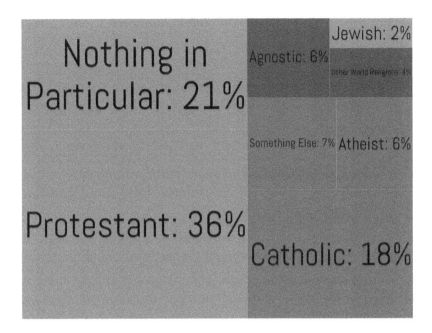

Figure 4.1. Size of Religious Traditions

Data from Cooperative Election Study. Stephen Ansolabehere, Brian F. Schaffner, and Sam Luks, Cambridge, MA: Harvard University, http://cces.gov.harvard.edu

which combine for another 18 percent of the population. But if we add those six groups together, that's nearly 95 percent of all Americans. That leaves the last 5 percent to a whole host of groups. Jews, Latter-day Saints, Buddhists, Muslims, Orthodox Christians, and Hindus combine to make up about one in twenty Americans.

Let's put that explanation in even more practical terms. For every Hindu on a survey, there are seventy-six Protestants and thirty-six Catholics. For every atheist, there are six Protestants. If you randomly sampled one hundred Americans, there would be two Jews in the sample and twenty nothing in particulars. Those smaller religious groups are an incredibly small part of the American religious landscape. That does not mean that they are not worth studying, it just means that they are incredibly hard to study in a rigorous way with the tools that we have available to us.

Let's say that someone asked me what seems like a perfectly reasonable question: How has the Latter-day Saints church attendance changed over the past several decades? I think that's a worthwhile question to ask. However, there is (to the best of my knowledge) no publicly available data that would allow me to answer that question with any statistical certainty. And figure 4.2 illustrates the problem I face.

The tall bars represent the number of Protestants that appears in each wave of the General Social Survey. The very short darker bars illustrate how many Latter-day Saints are in each wave of the GSS. As you can quickly tell, the disparity is tremendous and has huge implications for my ability as a social scientist to analyze how Latter-day Saints have engaged in political or religious behavior over the past four decades.

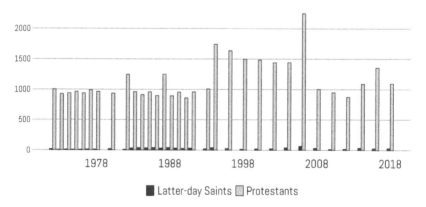

Figure 4.2. The Number of Latter-day Saints and Protestants in Each Wave of the GSS

Data from the General Social Survey, a project of the independent research organization NORC at the University of Chicago, with principal funding from the National Science Foundation, https://gss.norc.org/Get-The-Data

Looking at actual numbers helps to bring this point home. There have been thirty-two waves of the General Social Survey dating back to 1972, and a total of 64,814 respondents have been included in the sample. In that entire time, 834 respondents have indicated they were LDS. When the next wave of the GSS comes out, I can expect there to be about twenty-five Latter-day Saints in the sample compared to over a thousand Protestants. As a result of a very small sample size, it's essentially impossible to have an accurate view of LDS church attendance or Buddhists' voting preferences over a long time frame. We just don't have the ability to make assessments like that due to lack of data.

Why are social scientists so reluctant to report on findings from small sample sizes? It goes back to a term that many people throw out but don't fully understand: "statistical power." Think of it like this. You are the general manager of a baseball team, and you are interested in an exciting young hitter. But there's only one issue: he's taken only twenty-five at bats in a professional game. In those twenty-five plate appearances, he hit ten home runs. Would you be willing to sign him to a long-term multi-million-dollar contract? I think we would all hesitate just a bit and want to see him face a few more pitchers. Why? Because in the next twenty-five at bats he might strike out every time. Then your assessment of this prospect would change dramatically. The same issue arises when it comes to making pronouncements about how often Latter-day Saints attend church when there are only a few dozen in the sample. The GSS may have managed to randomly contact a disproportionately devout group, but we would never know that unless the sample grew exponentially and became more representative. Sure, a survey will produce results, but we just can't trust them that much.

This issue of small sample size and small religious groups converges during the run-up to a presidential election. Every large news agency in the United States partners with a survey firm to conduct a poll to get a sense of what candidate is leading and by how much. In recent years, these organizations have begun shifting their polls to focus on individual battleground states instead of just grabbing a random national sample. That strategy makes sense, given that the United States doesn't elect presidents based on popular vote. However, that strategy has had two ripple effects when it comes to understanding religion and politics.

The first is that polling data about how evangelicals in a swing state like Michigan are going to vote does not translate that well to the rest of the country. Even though we often talk about religious groups at the national level, there are significant regional variations. An evangelical in Michigan is not the same as an evangelical in Arizona or Florida, and to try to use data in one state to make pronouncements about voting behavior in another is fraught with problems.

The other consequence of moving to this state-level polling strategy is based on sample size. Most horse-race style national polls have about a thousand respondents. That's a solid number to generate good statistical power without spending too much money. But many of these state-level polls are smaller than that— lots of them poll only six hundred respondents. That decision is based more on finances than statistical power. Running a national poll of a thousand respondents is much cheaper than commissioning five state-level polls of six hundred each.

But in a poll of just six hundred respondents, it becomes much more difficult than in a poll of one thousand to cut the sample into subsets, such as only men or only Hispanics or only Catholics. Recall that in the general population about 20 percent of individuals identify as Roman Catholic. So a state-level poll of Pennsylvania may only yield 120 total Catholics. That's not enough to generate any real level of statistical power, and it's impossible to break Catholics down by gender when you have a sample that small.

When these polling outfits release their results to the general public, they usually offer two reports. The item you see on the news that says 55 percent of respondents favored the Republican while the Democrat was polling at 47 percent offers "top line" results. They are broad, eye-catching, and easy to convey on the nightly news. However, many polling firms release a second report called the cross-tabulations. This is where they list the vote intention by gender, race, and age. Many pundits love poring over these "cross-tabs" to gain insight on how each candidate is faring with a specific voting bloc. However, the religion section of cross-tabs usually stops at reporting white evangelicals and Catholics. Why? Because the polling firm knows that they don't have enough statistical power to list vote choice for groups like Latter-day Saints, Jews, or Hindus. It's not that they are biased against these groups, it's just that there's too much uncertainty surrounding these estimates.

However, there is good news on the horizon. Big data has come to the rescue in ways academics are only beginning to embrace. Up until 2006, researchers studying religion had only one true longitudinal data source: the aforementioned General Social Survey. Each year's survey averaged about two thousand respondents. The data was very high quality, but there wasn't a huge sample in each wave of the survey. But in recent years, switching surveys to an online format, rather than a face-to-face delivery mode, has dramatically reduced the cost of collecting data and may have actually increased the quality of those responses.

Remember, there were a total of 834 Latter-day Saints included in the forty-six years of the General Social Survey. In the first year of the Cooperative Election Study in 2006, there were 555, and another 592 were added just two years later. There have been four individual waves of the CES that contain more LDS respondents in that one year than the GSS had in all thirty-two waves combined (figure 4.3). In the combined CES

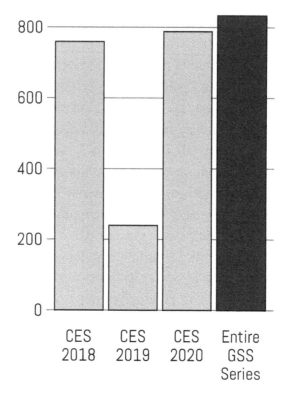

Figure 4.3. Number of Latter-day Saints in Each Sample

Data from the General Social Survey, a project of the independent research organization NORC at the University of Chicago, with principal funding from the National Science Foundation, https://gss.norc.org/Get-The-Data

Data from Cooperative Election Study. Stephen Ansolabehere, Brian F. Schaffner, and Sam Luks, Cambridge, MA: Harvard University, http://cces.gov.harvard.edu

there are 7,044 Latter-day Saints, a nearly ninefold increase over the GSS. And other surveys are being fielded all the time. The Nationscape Study surveyed six thousand respondents every week for eighteen months in the run-up to the 2020 presidential election. That sample alone contains over five thousand Latter-day Saints.

Thus, with survey data from the CES and Nationscape, research-ers will be able to answer questions that were unattainable when

I began graduate school in the mid-2000s. There will be dissertations written on the political behavior of Buddhists or whether Orthodox Christians go to church in patterns that are more similar to Protestants or Catholics. And, these huge data sources allow us to drill down into specific Protestant denominations. Now we have hundreds of Southern Baptists or United Methodists in a sample, not a few dozen.

CONCLUSIONS

I have to admit that I feel a tinge of sadness when I think about how many questions about the social, political, and religious world we will never be able to answer. If a social scientist is looking for data related to John F. Kennedy's election in 1960, I know of only one dataset that can provide that—the American National Election Study. But if someone wants to understand what share of white Southerners were Roosevelt supporters in 1932, there's no data that exists to answer that question. While I am grateful that we have a tremendous resource like the General Social Survey to help us understand nearly fifty years' worth of trends, it's hard to know how Catholic Church attendance has waxed and waned over American history. We just don't have the data to assess how religious the early colonists were when they came to the New World.

But I quickly move on from regret about what we can never know to what we can know about American religion in the near future. We now have the capability to ask and answer questions about how church attendance fades among the very oldest Americans. Or how religious devotion varies as several different generations age through the life cycle. I've always been slightly worried that I would run out of ideas for graphs to make or angles to pursue in the data, but every analysis I conduct and every news story I read leads to more ideas and new theories to test. There are always more things we can know.

But above all, I am so incredibly hopeful for those who will study American religion in the future. Many smaller religious groups often feel excluded and ignored by the academic community. I hope that I've made it clear that the reasons for this are not necessarily rooted in any sort of bias or prejudice but are instead the result of more practical concerns. But as more and more big datasets become publicly available, the excuses that scholars, pollsters, and journalists had for not discussing smaller religious groups are becoming more difficult to come by. We may be entering a new era of scholarship among American religion—one that is more nuanced and inclusive than we could have dreamed about just twenty years ago.

For Further Reading

Huff, Darrell. *How to Lie with Statistics*. New York: W. W. Norton & Company, 1954.

> In this classic book on teaching statistics or learning how to use them, Huff does a masterful job of showing how unscrupulous individuals can use statistical tricks or visual tweaks to change the implications of their analysis. I still reference this book from time to time when thinking about the best way to convey information.

Silver, Nate. *The Signal and the Noise: Why So Many Predictions Fail—but Some Don't*. New York: Penguin, 2012.

> Nate Silver may be the most well-known statistician alive today, having founded the website FiveThirtyEight and risen to fame by predicting Obama's election and reelection with startling accuracy. Silver's book is an in-depth description of

just why it's so difficult to make predictions and how easy it is to get lost chasing things in the data that end up being meaningless.

Wheelan, Charles. *Naked Statistics: Stripping the Dread from the Data*. New York: W. W. Norton & Company, 2013.

Statistics is not that fun for most people, and for many it appears to be completely incomprehensible. Charles Wheelan has a special gift of translating difficult statistical concepts into accessible prose. His examples are so good that I often assign parts of this book to my students who are taking research methods.

College leads young people away from religion

I'M BOTH A PASTOR AND A SOCIAL SCIENTIST, WHICH to me seems fairly mundane, because I've been doing both of those jobs most of my adult life. But when people, especially Christians, find out this fact, they are fascinated by the combination. I think many people assume academia is not particularly friendly to people of a religious persuasion, so they wonder how I could have spent enough time in higher education to become an academic and still claim to be a Christian—a Christian pastor, no less. While it's been my experience that academics tend to be less religious than the general population, it's not like I'm the only Christian professor on my campus. I've had very few encounters where I perceived any hostility to the fact that I lead a small Baptist church. In fact, the opposite response is more common—students, faculty, and staff seem to respect the fact that I wear both hats.

But my experience goes against how many Christians (especially evangelicals) seem to think about the religious environment on most college campuses. I am often asked by parents of teenagers who were raised in a religious environment how their son or daughter can maintain their faith when they send them off to some large state university or private liberal arts college. Many of them seem to believe that as soon as their child walks into a freshman class, they will throw out their Bibles and pick up Nietzsche.

It's not like they've plucked this idea out of thin air. It was the premise of a film released in 2014 called *God's Not Dead*, which became very popular in Christian circles and spawned two sequels. The premise of the first movie is that an evangelical student enrolls in a philosophy class led by an atheist professor. In order to pass the course, each student has to sign a declaration that "God is dead." The main character refuses, and this sets up a series of debates in the class about the existence of God. That last debate ends when most of the class sides with the student and the professor leaves in defeat.

With reinforcement such as this, the assumption that going to college leads to disaffiliation has put down deep roots in the psyche of many conservative Christians over the last few years. But is that even a valid assumption? Are people with higher levels of education more likely to say that they have no religious affiliation than those who have completed only high school?

Using data from twelve years of the CES, I calculated the share who identified as atheist, agnostic, and nothing in particular at six education levels, ranging from those with no high school diploma to respondents with graduate degrees. The results (visualized in figure 5.1) are clear and unambiguous in every wave of the dataset. Those with the least education are the most likely to indicate that they have no religious affiliation. In fact, the negative relationship between education and religious disaffiliation is maintained in all twelve years of the survey.

In 2008, 26 percent of those without a high school diploma identified as an atheist, agnostic, or nothing in particular. Only 19 percent of those with a graduate degree did. And that seven-point gap is fairly consistent across all years of the survey. In some cases, the gap does narrow, but it never gets smaller than three percentage points. However, it does grow to double digits

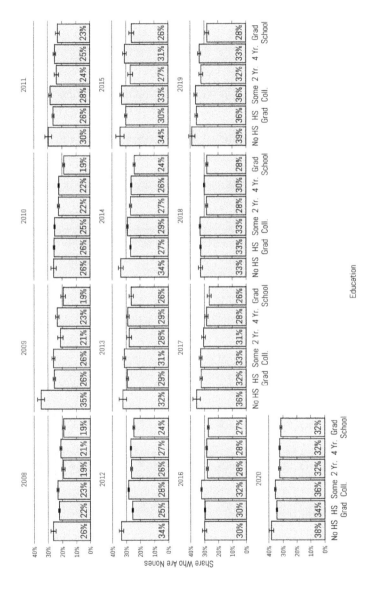

Figure 5.1. The Relationship between Education and Religious Affiliation

Data from Cooperative Election Study. Stephen Ansolabehere, Brian F. Schaffner, and Sam Luks, Cambridge, MA: Harvard University, http://cces.gov.harvard.edu

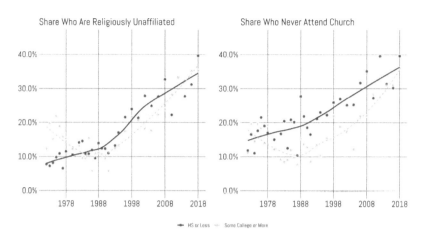

Figure 5.2. The Religiosity of 18- to 30-Year-Olds Divided by College Experience

Data from the General Social Survey, a project of the independent research organization NORC at the University of Chicago, with principal funding from the National Science Foundation, https://gss.norc.org/Get-The-Data

in four waves of the survey. This is strong evidence that higher levels of education are actually positively related to a religious affiliation.

But this doesn't tell the whole story about the role of college in the spiritual life of young people. The people in that sample could have received their college degree decades ago in a time when American society was perhaps more religious overall. So to test the impacts of college more directly, I restricted my sample to just eighteen- to thirty-year-old respondents and split it into two groups: those who had not gone beyond a high school diploma and those who had taken at least a few college courses. The panel on the left of figure 5.2 is the share of each group who say that they have no religious affiliation, while the panel on the right shows the share who report that they never attend religious services. While there's certainly overlap between those who never attend church and those who claim no religious affiliation, there are significant numbers of young people who never go to church but still claim a religious attachment. In data from the last decade, over a third of young people who never attend church still claim a religious affiliation.

In the early 1970s, it's fair to say that those who went to college were more likely than those with a high school diploma or less to be religiously unaffiliated and more likely to report never-attending services. However, by the late 1980s the narrative began to change completely. Around 1988, young people who had gone to college were slightly less likely to indicate that they were a religious none. And if those lines are traced from the late 1980s to 2014, there's no evidence that more highly educated young people are more likely to have no religious affiliation. The current trend line does point to a future when young people with some college experience are less likely to be religious, but that hasn't arrived just yet.

In terms of church attendance, the gap between those who did and did not go to college is much larger. For instance, in 1988 just 10 percent of young people who went to college reported never-attending church. For those who stopped at high school it was closer to 20 percent. And this attendance gap remains significant for several decades. By 2008, it had narrowed somewhat to seven points and that gap has completely disappeared in the most recent wave of the General Social Survey. Thus, there's some evidence that young people with higher levels of education may in the future be leaving religion at a rate that exceeds those with a high school diploma, but that's clearly not been the case for the past forty-six years.

All of this comes into clearer focus when looking at the distribution of religious traditions among the youngest Americans, divided by those who stopped at high school and those who went on to take at least some college courses. In data from the 2020 Cooperative Election Study, there's unmistakable evidence that the type of experience where a professor convinces young people

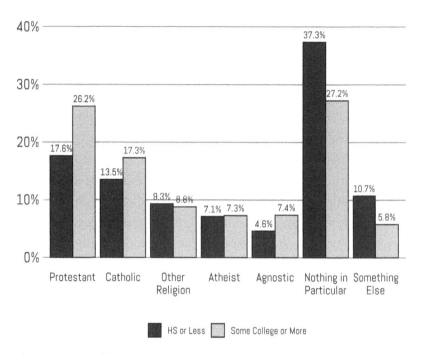

Figure 5.3. Religious Makeup of 18- to 25-Year-Olds

Data from Cooperative Election Study. Stephen Ansolabehere, Brian F. Schaffner, and Sam Luks, Cambridge, MA: Harvard University, http://cces.gov.harvard.edu

to believe in God that was dramatized in *God's Not Dead* is not truly representative of what is happening in the real world.

According to this data visualized in figure 5.3, young people who pursued higher education are nine percentage points more likely to indicate that they are Protestant and five points more likely to say that they are Catholic than those who ended their education at high school. There's no difference between the percentage of the two groups who say they are atheist (both are around 7 percent). Those identifying as agnostic are slightly more prevalent among those with higher levels of education—7 percent compared to 5 percent. However, the most noteworthy difference is the share that professes that their religion is "nothing in particular." Just 27 percent of those with higher education chose this response option, while over 37 percent of those who had a high school diploma or less did. In fact, "nothing in particular" was far and away the most popular choice among the low-education group. They were nearly three times more likely to choose this option than say they were Catholic. But it's also worth pointing out that only a single percentage point separated the share of college educated young people who identified as Protestants (26 percent) and those who identified as "nothing in particular" (27 percent).

CONCLUSIONS

For many parents of teenagers, the thought of sending their children off to a university where they won't have someone reminding them to go to class, get enough sleep, and brush their teeth is a terrifying prospect. That can be especially true when those parents have raised their child in a specific faith tradition and want to make sure that this part of their family culture is passed down to the next generation. However, according to the data, there seems to be little evidence that college, in and of itself, is turning legions of committed Christians into godless heathens.

Other scholars, using a variety of well-crafted research designs, reinforce this finding. For instance, two sociologists, Damon Mayrl (Colby College) and Jeremy Eucker (Baylor University), used an ideal data source to test this exact hypothesis. The survey asked questions of young people between the ages of thirteen and seventeen in 2002. Then the research team recontacted that same group in 2005 and again in 2008, thus making it possible to assess how young people's views of the world changed at the individual level. When looking specifically at how those respondents' religious views changed over time, they found that those who went to college were no more or less likely to embrace an impersonal or uninvolved view of God than those who did not decide to further their education. In fact, the authors found that on some dimensions of religious belief, including believing in God, young people who went to college were less likely to express doubts than those who did not continue their education.

Mayrl and Eucker concluded that the mechanisms through which the college experience impacted the views of young people were not necessarily the professors, the readings, and the coursework, but instead the social contexts that young people find themselves in when they go to college. Consider what percentage of time the average student actually spends in the lecture hall, a professor's office, or the library during their college career and compare that to the number of hours they spend in their dorm room, the dining hall, or at informal gatherings of friends. Paul Musgrave, a political scientist, once tweeted, "As a professor, Fox News tells me I can turn my students into Communists, and experience tells me I can't even make them do the readings." I think if you read that sentence to most professors, they would begin nodding their head vigorously in agreement.

So if the person leading the lecture is not the one having a huge impact on the religious and political views of young people, then who is? According to research released in 2020, it's their roommates. Because young people are typically randomly assigned a roommate their freshman year, this new living situation becomes somewhat of an experiment in social influence. When a research team led by Logan Strother surveyed those freshmen several times over the course of the fall and spring semesters, they found something that shouldn't be that surprising to us—the political ideology of each respondent started moving closer to that of their roommate. Spending two or three hours a week with a college professor doesn't hold a candle to spending hundreds of hours with a roommate.

It pains me to say this, but I don't have that much influence over the students in my courses. But that doesn't mean college doesn't change them. Looked at in its entirety, the college experience may actually make college students even more sure of what they believe when they finally graduate. There's a theory in the communication literature called the inoculation effect. This is the idea that when someone is confronted with several weaker attacks on their beliefs, they become more prepared to defend those beliefs when they come under serious attacks. This is essentially how a vaccine works—it gives an individual a weakened version of the virus, so that when the immune system encounters the real thing, it can easily fight off the villain.

Challenging a young person on what they believe in a supportive, open environment may be just the kind of test a teenager needs to really consider what they believe. Then, when the bigger challenges of life come along, they are better prepared to hold firm to their convictions. As a parent myself, I completely understand the tendency to shelter our children. But college comes at an ideal time in the life cycle for young people to venture out and engage with people who don't look like them, live like them, or believe like them. Exposing our teenagers to new ideas and new cultures is one of the most powerful things we can do for the next generation.

For Further Reading

Mayrl, Damon, and Jeremy E. Uecker. "Higher Education and Religious Liberalization among Young Adults." *Social Forces* 90, no. 1 (2011): 181–208.

As mentioned in this chapter, Mayrl and Uecker dispel the notion that college has a deleterious impact on the religious faith of young people. Their data is robust and their methods are well chosen—all driving home a central point: getting a university education doesn't lead people away from religion.

Schwadel, Philip. "Birth Cohort Changes in the Association between College Education and Religious Non-Affiliation." *Social Forces* 93, no. 2 (2014): 719–46.

In this article, Schwadel describes how the impact of a college education on a person's faith has changed over time. This work carefully considers how the increased secularization of society may have unexpected consequences for the relationship between education and religion.

Strother, Logan, Spencer Piston, Ezra Golberstein, Sarah E. Gollust, and Daniel Eisenberg. "College Roommates Have a Modest but Significant Influence on Each Other's Political Ideology." *Proceedings of the National Academy of Sciences* 118, no. 2 (2021).

One of the most important tools a social scientist can use is a good experiment. The fact that young people are often randomly assigned roommates their freshmen year of college provided the authors an ideal way to test the assumption that professors can change the political beliefs of students. As mentioned in the chapter, it's not the professors doing the persuading, it's other students on campus.

Nondenominational
Christians are rare

ONE OF THE BEST THINGS ABOUT THE INTERNET IS
that anyone can find their own little corner of cyberspace and
learn more about it every day. That's absolutely the case with
people who are interested in understanding religion. There's an
entire ecosystem of news outlets that focus solely on the intersection of religion and society, both in the United States and abroad.
On top of that, hundreds of scholars, theologians, and lay people
on social media aggregate information about religion and dis-
seminate it to their followers.

I'm usually asked once or twice a week to comment on a story
or provide background about a trend by a reporter. I really enjoy
doing it, and it's given me a unique insight into the industry. One
thing that I have come to understand about the media business
is that the thing that separates the good journalists from the
great ones is that great journalists have built up a huge network
of sources. When a story breaks, they know exactly who to call
in order to understand what's happening.

Building up a strong network of trusted sources is a form of
currency for reporters. Many in the news business have forged
these relationships over decades of meticulous reporting on the
happenings in American religion. During a typical year, certain

events play a prominent role in what gets covered by religion reporters. For instance, religious holidays such as Christmas, Easter, Passover, and Ramadan get covered extensively. However, other smaller events punctuating the calendar year also seem to get a lot of coverage. One example of that is denominational meetings.

The Southern Baptist Convention (SBC) holds an annual get-together where tens of thousands of members convene to network, hear from prominent leaders in the Convention, and vote on resolutions the SBC might adopt for the coming year. The United Methodist Church (UMC) organizes a general conference each year, as well. The meetings are similar to the Southern Baptist Convention, with speakers, committees, and votes on the future of the denomination taking center stage. Both events are covered extensively in the media and can give the impression to a casual observer that the Protestant universe revolves around the happenings of these large denominations.

But there's been a slow and steady shift occurring in Protestant Christianity that many people who don't pay close attention to American religion might miss—denominations are rapidly fading in importance and are being replaced by thousands of nondenominational churches all across the United States. These nondenominational churches have become one of the most important forces in American religion but have avoided the media spotlight.

When media outlets cover an event at one of these nondenominational churches, they treat it almost like an aberration—as if somehow this group has drifted away from the denominational mothership and doesn't really exemplify what's going on in Protestant Christianity. But these types of churches are clearly not outliers in the data. They are increasingly becoming the norm in many communities.

Before addressing the meteoric rise of nondenominational Christians, it's worthwhile to take a look at how denominational Protestants have declined in the past several decades. For most scholars of American religion, the two most important denominational bodies are the aforementioned Southern Baptist Convention and United Methodist Church. The Southern Baptist Convention is the largest Protestant denomination in the United States at just over 14 million members and receives a great deal of attention from religion journalists. The Convention has become the symbol of evangelical Christianity in the United States, and debates inside the SBC are often seen as emblematic of all of evangelicalism. Southern Baptists are obviously concentrated in the Southern portion of the United States, but there are SBC churches in many parts of the country.

While the Southern Baptist Convention is the embodiment of the evangelical movement, the United Methodist Church represents mainline Christianity. Mainline Protestants are less conservative than evangelicals. Denominations in the mainline allow women to be pastors, and many of them are open and affirming to LGBT individuals. The United Methodists are far and away the largest of the mainline traditions at 6.5 million members. They are also one of the most geographically dispersed denominations in the United States. An anecdote floats around religious circles that every county in the United States has a UMC congregation. While that may not be technically true, the sentiment is that the United Methodists are everywhere.

While the Southern Baptists and the United Methodists may not share many commonalities in their theology, they are alike on one crucial dimension: both enjoyed tremendous and sustained growth for most of American history but are now facing a steep decline in membership, as can be seen in figure 6.1.

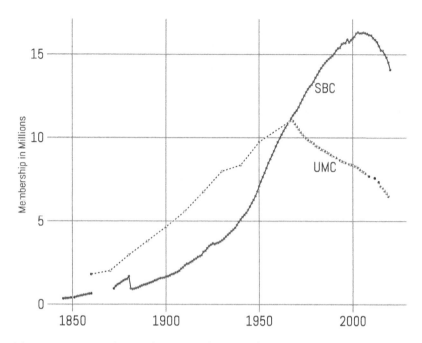

Figure 6.1. Total Members of the Southern Baptist Convention and the United Methodist Church

Data compiled from membership reports published by the Southern Baptist Convention and United Methodist Church.

The United Methodists counted just under five million members in 1900 and nearly doubled in size by 1950. However, the exponential growth slowed significantly in the following decades, with United Methodists hitting their peak membership in 1967 at just over eleven million members. That peak was fueled by a merger of the Methodist Church with the Evangelical United Brethren Church. By 1975, their membership had dropped below ten million. They lost another million United Methodists by 1987, and the downward curve steepened from there. According to data from 2019, about 6.5 million Americans were members of a United Methodist congregation, a decline of over 40 percent from their peak.

The Southern Baptist Convention experienced growth that was more sustained than the United Methodists'. They hit five million members around 1940 and then doubled in size by 1962. By the late 1960s the SBC enjoyed a membership that was larger than the United Methodist Church, and by 1990 there were over fifteen million Southern Baptists. The peak year for Southern Baptist membership was 2006 at 16.3 million. However, they have faced a steep decline from that point forward. Between 2006 and 2016, they lost over a million members, and by 2020 their total membership was about 14.1 million. While the Southern Baptists are obviously larger than the United Methodists, it's interesting to note that between 2006 and 2020, the SBC lost more members than the United Methodists did. Yet as a percentage the United Methodists sustained a larger percentage decline compared to the Southern Baptists (18 percent vs. 14 percent).

In 2003, a total of 24.5 million Americans were on the membership rolls of the Southern Baptist Convention or the United Methodist Church. Just sixteen years later nearly four million fewer people were members of either tradition. This same pattern is repeated in other Protestant traditions as well. In the 1960s, there were 3.4 million Episcopalians, and in 2019 that number was 1.6 million members—a decline of more than half. It's not hyperbolic to say that denominational Protestant Christianity is facing a rapid collapse in members and an uncertain future.

That exodus from the Protestant ranks shows up in survey data from the past twelve years, as well. The CES asked people who identified as Protestant what denominational family they affiliated with and offered them a dozen response options from Baptist to Methodist to Episcopalian. Comparing data from 2008 to 2020 in figure 6.2 paints a fairly bleak picture for many Protestant traditions.

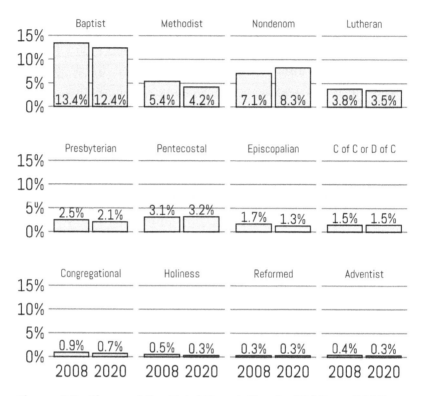

Figure 6.2. Share of the Total Population in 2008 vs. 2020

Data from Cooperative Election Study. Stephen Ansolabehere, Brian F. Schaffner, and Sam Luks, Cambridge, MA: Harvard University, http://cces.gov.harvard.edu

The share of Americans who identify as Baptist dropped from 13.4 percent in 2008 to 12.4 percent in 2020. Methodists saw an even larger decline during the same period (5.4 percent to 4.2 percent). Lutherans decreased in size, along with Presbyterians and Episcopalians. The share of Americans who identified with those four traditions combined dropped by nearly three percentage points in just over a decade. That translates to about ten million fewer Americans who are Methodists, Baptists, Presbyterians, or Episcopalians.

There's one clear outlier in the graph—those who identify as nondenominational. While Baptists and Methodists both experienced a decline of at least a percentage point, nondenominational Christians went the other direction. In 2008, 7.1 percent of Americans were nondenominational. By 2020, that had jumped to 8.3 percent. In 2020, there were nearly twice as many nondenominational Christians as Methodists. It's the only Protestant tradition that grew in a meaningful way over the past twelve years.

But when the timeline is expanded even further, the true magnitude of the shift in Protestant Christianity comes into fuller view, as visualized in figure 6.3. The General Social Survey has been asking questions about religious affiliation since 1972. In the

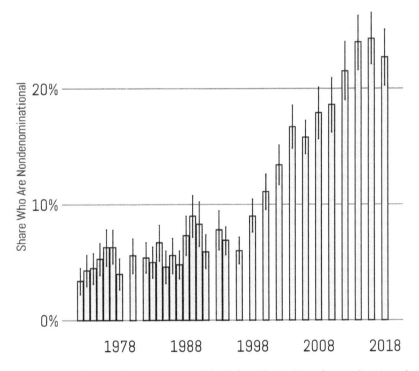

Figure 6.3. Share of Protestants Who Identify as Nondenominational

Data from the General Social Survey, a project of the independent research organization NORC at the University of Chicago, with principal funding from the National Science Foundation, https://gss.norc.org/Get-The-Data

very first wave of the GSS, there were 1,613 respondents, and just over a thousand of them were Protestants. When asked what type of denomination they were affiliated with, just 36 people said that they were nondenominational Christians. To be blunt, nondenominational Christianity was nothing more than a rounding error in the 1970s. Even if scholars were interested in studying this group through quantitative data, there wasn't a sufficient sample to do so.

However, the share of Protestants who identified as nondenominational began to gradually increase through the 1990s, as can be seen in figure 12.1. By 1998, slightly fewer than one in ten Protestants identified as nondenominational. The share essentially doubled over the next ten years. By 2012, about 22 percent of American Protestants were nondenominational. In other words, about a quarter of Protestant Christianity is no longer associated with an established denomination.

While the General Social Survey's estimate of the number of nondenominational Christians in the United States is a bit higher than the one derived from the CES, there's ample evidence to support the conclusion that just about one in ten Americans today identifies as a nondenominational Christian. That means that in 2020, the number of nondenominational Christians is likely the same size as the membership of the Southern Baptist Convention and the United Methodist Church combined.

CONCLUSIONS

The rise of the nondenominationals has generated a whole host of problems for those who study and write about American religion. To return to the discussion of media coverage of religion, it's clear why many religion journalists write stories about large denominational meetings. They are well-organized, something newsworthy usually happens when those denominations get together, and many journalists have close relationships with those in leadership in established denominations. Reporters who cover religion know the back stories, the culture, and the future challenges facing these denominational bodies.

When it comes to nondenominational Christianity, however, everything is turned upside down. Religion journalists cannot cover their annual convention, because these churches don't have one. Many nondenominational churches have existed for just ten or twenty years and thus journalists looking for a back story don't have a great deal of history to draw upon. As a group, nondenominationals are fragmented, disconnected, and amorphous. While these traits seem to be key reasons many of them are growing, these factors also make them a nightmare to report on. General news followers aren't going to hear as much about these churches as they do about major denominations, so the public has a skewed perception of their numbers.

At the same time, they pose challenges for academic researchers who are trying to study this new movement in an empirically rigorous way. The structure of surveys doesn't necessarily lend itself to sorting nondenominationals into categories. For instance, if a respondent says they are Methodist, most survey instruments will follow up by asking what type of Methodist they are, with options such as United Methodist, Free Methodist, or African Methodist Episcopal. There's no straightforward way to ask a follow-up question of someone who identifies as nondenominational. Because of this, most scholars place all nondenominationals into one category.

Nondenominational churches are the ultimate expression of the "bottom up" shift that's happened in many aspects of American society in the past several years. The widespread adoption of social media has moved the locus of power to the grass roots. Nondenominationals have no hierarchy like the United Methodists or even the Southern Baptists. Many of them began organically with a few families meeting in homes and grew from there. And to use a term that has become ubiquitous on social media—those house churches went viral. There are countless stories of nondenominational churches starting out with twenty people and growing to two thousand in a year or two. Many of these pastors in these rapidly growing nondenominational churches have no theological training or formal ordination. Gatekeepers in traditional denominations would have never given them the opportunity to stand in a pulpit, and now these religious entrepreneurs have built up their own churches, sometimes with followings in the tens of thousands.

In the same way, many of the most prominent voices on social media got their start by picking up a phone and making a video, taking a picture, or sending a tweet. No one asked about their education, qualifications, or background before they were allowed to post on social media. If people found their content to be compelling, they hit the "follow" button. These influencers didn't need a major media company or television network to financially support them. For most, their growth has been completely organic. In essence, social media democratized the information landscape and led to a more diverse array of voices being heard, and nondenominational churches did the same for Protestant Christianity. While it's not possible to isolate one clear cause for the rise in nondenominational Christianity, social media surely contributed to its accelerated growth.

It's important to note that there are significant downsides to this new arrangement, however. The term "gatekeeping" has a negative connotation, but there are times when giving everyone a platform may not be a good thing. We all have heard stories of people gaining huge online followings by encouraging racist, sexist, and xenophobic views. During the height of the Covid-19 pandemic, a video called "The Plandemic" went viral on social media. It was filled with falsehoods about the virus and unfounded allegations that Covid-19 was the result of a coordinated effort by world governments to take away freedoms from average Americans. Despite the best efforts of the largest social networks to have the video removed, it was viewed over eight million times on various platforms.

At the same time, it doesn't take many internet searches to find videos of nondenominational church pastors delivering a Sunday sermon that contains information that is either factually incorrect or downright heretical to most mainstream Christians. While many denominational leaders would agree that having some type of formal training in theology is not an absolute prerequisite for pastoring a church, it certainly doesn't hurt.

In the future, both journalists and scholars of American religion will have to develop new analytical tools and construct a new framework for understanding the structure and order of American Protestant Christianity. Measuring the success of a church by number of people in the pews may be replaced by number of times the service was viewed on Facebook or YouTube. Tracking the social media following of pastors may become the most effective way to assess the impact and reach that he or she is having on American Christianity. These new churches are harder to track, more difficult to organize, and potentially impossible to characterize. That means that social science is more than likely undercounting the share of the American population that is nondenominational right now. Unless better survey questions are constructed, we will likely be presented with a more distorted view of American Christianity as each year passes.

For Further Reading

Christerson, Brad, and Richard Flory. *The Rise of Network Christianity: How Independent Leaders Are Changing the Religious Landscape.* Oxford: Oxford University Press, 2017.

Christerson and Flory provide one of the most in-depth academic explorations of the causes and consequences of nondenominational Christianity. While the focus is largely on charismatic churches, the authors explain how Americans have become averse to institutions over time and how this has led to the decline of denominational Christianity.

Dochuk, Darren. *From Bible Belt to Sunbelt: Plain-folk Religion, Grassroots Politics, and the Rise of Evangelical Conservatism.* New York: W. W. Norton & Company, 2010.

Darren Dochuk tracks the history of the great American evangelical migration from Southern states such as Oklahoma and Arkansas to Southern California throughout the 1960s and 1970s. While not explicitly about nondenominational Christianity, Dochuk's observations about how the culture of the West coast impacted the evolution of American evangelicalism help to explain the current state of Protestant Christianity.

Shellnut, Kate. "The Key to This Church Planting Network's Success? Start Big, Stay Big." *Christianity Today*. June 21, 2019, https://www.christianitytoday.com/ct/2019/july-august/arc-association-related-churches-church-planting-launch.html. Accessed: July 6, 2021.

One of the most important organizations in the world of nondenominational Christianity is the Association of Related Churches (ARC). Shellnut describes how this church planting network has been so successful at starting new churches all across the United States. The details about funding, equipping, and launching new churches offer a window into how these organizations operate.

Born-again experiences are common and dramatically change a person's life

I GREW UP IN A TYPICAL SOUTHERN BAPTIST CHURCH in the 1990s during the height of the evangelical movement in the United States. When you are raised in the Southern Baptist tradition, you quickly learn that these churches take the Great Commission seriously. The number of baptisms was tallied and reported on a weekly basis in the bulletin. A successful church was one where the pastor's hip waders were in constant use. Thus, a pastor was gauged largely on his ability to get people to the altar as the service drew to a close.

As I got older, I began to notice that the length of the invitational time (aka, the altar call) was directly proportional to how many people came forward. If the pianist got to the third verse of "Just As I Am" and no one had managed to find their way down front, I knew that my chances of beating the Catholics to my favorite restaurant were slim. The pastor would gaze scornfully at the restless congregation and inevitably give the signal to the worship leader to sing another verse and then another. I don't know how many stanzas there are to "I Surrender All" in the hymn book, but we managed to sing eight or nine on some Sundays.

I came to understand that salvation is a radical shift, that it produces dramatic changes in a person. The power of salvation was so profound that drunks would leave the bottle behind, drug addicts would set the needle down and never take it back up, and people who wanted to divorce their spouse would reconcile and recommit to their marriage once God had given them a new heart. Conversion was always compared to the life-altering experience that Paul had on the road to Damascus. He was on his way to persecute early Christians, but after meeting God on the road, his life was dramatically changed, and he became the most important figure in early Christianity.

Even in my youth, though, I often wondered, are those radical "born-again" experiences common? And do people really completely turn their lives around when they come forward and say the Sinner's prayer—the way they talk about when they give their testimony during the worship service? The impression that those sitting in the congregation of my Baptist church were left with was that to be saved was to be irrevocably changed—that a return to a prior lifestyle was not possible for those who had truly accepted Jesus in their heart.

But do such experiences stand up to empirical scrutiny? Unfortunately for all those traveling evangelists who seek to replicate these dramatic moments, I don't find much evidence in the data that they are common. Instead, I am left with two key findings. The first is that adults rarely report that they have undergone a born-again experience. The other is that, in almost all cases, their religious behavior did not change in any meaningful way after they went forward and asked Jesus into their heart.

Answering questions about individual changes in behavior is notoriously difficult. Most of the surveys I use for this book and in my other academic work are just not suited to the task. They don't ask the same people the same questions over a long period of time. Instead, they ask a new group of individuals a similar series of questions every year or two, which means tracking individual conversion is impossible using this data. However, social scientists do have other tools in our methodological toolbox to answer questions like this: one such tool is called panel data. Instead of the survey administrators sampling a new population in each wave of the survey, in a panel design the research team contacts the same people every time they go into the field. Usually this is done over a long period of time. For instance, the National Survey of Children interviewed their study group for the first time when they were 7 to 11 years old, the same group of young people were reinterviewed when they were 11 to 16, and finally when they were 17 to 22 years of age. This method gives researchers tremendous insight into what factors drive different outcomes among young people as they enter into adulthood. But panel data is not only used by academics. Often private research firms conduct weekly panels during the run-up to a presidential election, trying to isolate what factors lead voters to change their minds about who they will support for office.

Panel data is tremendously valuable to our understanding of the social world, but that's not to say that these surveys are without their faults. The biggest thing that we have to worry about when conducting a panel study is called survey attrition. Put simply, people drop out of these studies all the time. They get bored answering the questions, they move away and don't share their contact information, or in some cases they die. This is especially problematic because although the initial wave of a panel survey could have a strong, random sample, attrition never happens randomly. What that means is that the final wave of a panel may be 80 percent female, or have a huge share of elderly respondents, resulting in a group that's obviously not truly representative of the American public. There are ways to correct for this by using survey weights, but they can only do so much if the attrition rate rises exponentially and in ways that bias the sample too much to make it usable.

Despite these caveats, however, panel data is especially well suited to understanding the frequency of people having a born-again experience and how their behavior changes directly after such an important event in their lives. The Democracy Fund's Voter Study Group conducted a long-term panel survey that began in 2011 and 2012 and continued to contact participants periodically through January 2019. Using this data, we can track the number of Americans who indicated that they were not born-again but then changed their answer to that question at some point during the study period.

Across the seven-year time frame, stability is much more commonplace than a change in born-again status, as can be seen in figure 7.1. About 70 percent of the sample was not born-again at the beginning of the panel study and did not report being born-again in January 2019. On the other end of the spectrum, 23 percent of the sample indicated that they were born-again during the first collection period as well as the last collection period of the study. Thus, together these two groups represent

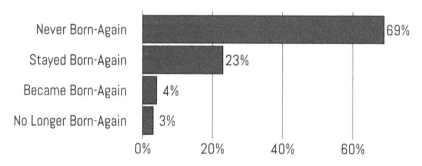

Figure 7.1. Comparing Born-Again Status in 2012 and 2019

Data from the VOTER (Views of the Electorate Research Survey), administered by the Democracy Fund's Voter Study Group. Los Angeles: University of California. https://www.voterstudygroup.org/data

92 percent of all Americans. That leaves only 4 percent who said that they became born-again during the eight-year time period, while 3 percent said that they were born-again at the beginning but not at the end.

Having established that the share of adults who become born-again over a nearly eight-year period is incredibly small, we can now turn to an even more important question: Of those who do indicate they have recently had a born-again experience, how does behavior differ in the wake of that change? From the countless stories of people sharing their testimonies during church services I have attended, I would assume that church attendance would spike after a conversion experience. If one is trying to find evidence of a dramatic life change, church attendance would be the first place to look. Again, the data does not bear that out.

I sorted the dataset to include only people who were not born-again in one wave but switched to a born-again identity in the next wave of the panel study. Then I took a look at their church attendance in the wave where they had indicated a change to a born-again status. I then did a quick calculation of church attendance change. To do that, I compared their self-reported church attendance right before they became born-again to their church attendance after they became born-again. If their attendance increased one level (say going from yearly to monthly or never to seldom attending), I categorized that as a small increase. However, if their attendance jumped at least two levels (e.g., going from monthly to more than once a week), then I classified that as a large increase. I also did the same comparison for people who indicated that their attendance declined after becoming born-again.

The first finding that stands out in figure 7.2 is that for a majority of respondents who became born-again, their overall level of church attendance did not change at all. Three in five people who became born-again were attending church just as

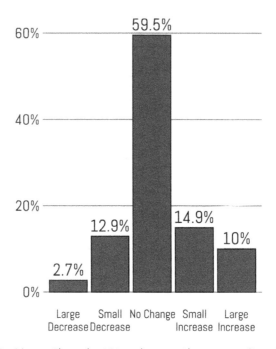

Figure 7.2. How Church Attendance Changes after Becoming Born-Again

Data from the VOTER (Views of the Electorate Research Survey), administered by the Democracy Fund's Voter Study Group. Los Angeles: University of California.https://www.voterstudygroup.org/data

often after they had the conversion experience. Thus, the radical change in behavior that many would expect doesn't appear in this data. However, that's not to say that there aren't some attendance changes for people who become born-again. In total, about 15 percent of those who turn their lives over to Jesus increase their church attendance by one level, and another 10 percent report church attendance that increases by at least two levels after the conversion.

Yet, what tempers these results is the fact that nearly 16 percent of people who said they had become born-again reported their church attendance actually dropped after that experience.

This obviously provides some sober evidence that the perception many evangelicals have of the born-again moment is not reflected in the lives of the average American. If looked at in totality, over three-quarters of people who became born-again do not report that their church attendance increased at all after that pivotal moment in their lives.

It's important that I point out here the limitations of data like this. First, it focuses on only adults in the United States. There's plenty of evidence that adult conversions are only a fraction of the total number of born-again events that happen in the United States. For instance, Barna reports that 64 percent of people become born-again before their eighteenth birthday, and another 13 percent made that commitment between eighteen and twenty-one years old. Additionally, while panel data is good, it's not perfect. We can only rely on our survey respondents understanding the questions completely and responding to them honestly. For instance, in this data, half of people who said that they identified as born-again indicated that they never attended church either before or after the conversion experience.

CONCLUSIONS

The fun part about being a social scientist is that it's my job to try to understand why people do the things they do. The maddening part about being a social scientist is that often people have no idea why they do what they do. Some people who indicated a change in their born-again status on a panel survey may have had a stereotypical conversion experience at a prayer meeting or a tent revival. But others may have just been moving through the survey quickly and made a careless mistake in how they answered these questions. It's impossible to know the frequency of either occurrence with complete accuracy. However, in the aggregate, I believe these types of surveys give a (sometimes blurry) picture of how the average person thinks about matters of religious concern.

I was always taught that religious conversion is a simple "on-off" light switch. Think of those famous lines of "Amazing Grace": "I once was lost but now I'm found, was blind but now I see." However, it doesn't appear that's always the case. Instead, a more apt metaphor might be a dimmer switch: sometimes a person moves closer to religion and their survey answers reflect that, and sometimes they move further away and they report no longer being born-again or that their church attendance declines. Thus, many people don't go from complete blindness to perfect vision, but most find themselves somewhere between the two.

For Further Reading

Burge, Ryan P. "Is Becoming Born-Again a Transformative Experience? Results from Three Sets of Panel Data." *Review of Religious Research* 63, no. 1 (2021): 83–105.

This is a more in-depth exploration of the topic of religious conversion from an academic perspective. Going beyond the information conveyed in this chapter, it focuses on how the political partisanship of newly converted Christians changes. When demographic factors are controlled for in a statistical model, there's no discernible change in political partisanship.

Patrikios, Stratos. "Self-stereotyping as 'Evangelical Republican': An empirical test." *Politics and Religion* 6, no. 4 (2013): 800–22.

The author tests how closely linked the terms "evangelical" and "Republican" have become in the minds of Americans. The results indicate that for those who are politically engaged, these two concepts have become fused in political discourse.

Webb, Stephen H. *Dylan Redeemed: from Highway 61 to Saved.* New York: Continuum, 2006.

When conducting research to write this chapter, I came across an interesting anecdote: the musician Bob Dylan experienced a supernatural conversion to Christianity while in a hotel room in 1978. That experience changed the course of his music and his career—and this book outlines that process in detail.

MYTH 8

You have to go to church frequently to be an evangelical

LET'S SAY THAT I ASKED YOU TO BE PART OF A SUR-vey that I was conducting. I take you into a room with a simple table and chair. I slide a manila folder across to you and tell you that when I leave the room I want you to open the folder and respond to the question on the paper. I leave, and you quickly pull out the piece of paper and see a single three-word question written across the top: "Who are you?"

What would be the first thing that crosses your mind when you are confronted with such an important philosophical question? Obviously not everyone uses the same thought process to come up with an answer. But trying to understand the thought process that you undertake to answer such a query is one of the most important puzzles facing social science. Having a firmer grasp of how individuals think about themselves and the rest of society is key in understanding concepts such as human motivation, group dynamics, and collective behavior.

There's no clear schema among academics about how human beings "make meaning" out of their lives, but one of the most well-known frameworks was established by Ruth Benedict, a pathbreaking anthropologist and a true leader of her academic discipline. Her 1946 book, *The Chrysanthemum and the Sword*, is considered to be one of the most influential and disputed texts about how societies influence individuals' view of themselves.[18]

When the book was released, many Americans were struggling to understand some of the stories that they were hearing from GIs returning from the Pacific theater about the behavior of the Japanese soldiers. Tales of Japanese infantrymen refusing to put down their weapons and fighting to the death even when they were outnumbered ten to one or Japanese kamikaze pilots intentionally flying their planes into American ships were incomprehensible for many Americans. Benedict was able to explain the behavior of the Japanese people in wartime by comparing their culture to that of the United States.

For Benedict, the Japanese answered the question, "Who Am I?" using a psychological and sociological framework entirely different from that of their American counterparts. In studying the literature by Japanese authors and news stories coming out of Japan, alongside extensive interviews she conducted with Japanese-Americans, Benedict argued that the Japanese live in what she dubbed "a shame culture." For the Japanese, the factor that guides the way they think about themselves is how other people in their community view them. Thus, meaning is not made by the individual, it is constructed by the society at large. Benedict believed that the reason Japanese pilots intentionally ended their lives by flying their aircraft into American warships was that to do anything else would bring shame to them and their families.

On the other hand, Benedict believed that the United States was based on "guilt culture." In this type of society, the way that people make decisions about what to do is not based on how other people view them, but instead on how they view themselves. In essence, Benedict argues that Americans construct their view of self largely through psychological avenues, while for the Japanese this process is more sociological. To use a simple example, if an American saw a large sum of money on the street, before picking it up they would think, "Can I live with myself if I pick up this cash?" while the Japanese thought process would be, "Will anyone ever find out that I picked up this money?"

Obviously, Benedict's view of the Japanese and American cultures has been roundly criticized by scholars from a variety of social science backgrounds. Her work is, at best, incredibly reductive and, at worst, patently racist. To try to encapsulate all the cultural nuances of millions of people through interviewing a few citizens, reading newspapers, and watching some films is going to gloss over many details about what it means to be American or Japanese.

While Benedict's binary view of shame culture versus guilt culture has largely been left behind, many social scientists have used her basic framework to help us understand how human beings construct their sense of identity. From an academic perspective, we understand that most individuals perceive themselves using aspects of both guilt culture and shame culture. That is, sometimes we lean on our own thought patterns and psychological processes to understand who we are, but other times we judge our self-worth sociologically, thinking carefully about how others perceive us.

Those frameworks collide when social scientists seek the most accurate way to conceptualize religiosity, a problem with which they have grappled for decades. The way most of us who study religion try to articulate this conceptualization of religion is a schema called "intrinsic versus extrinsic religiosity." The intrinsic dimension, sometimes called a vertical orientation, presupposes that religion is primarily about the relationship an individual has with the Divine. Thus, the focus of study here is a person's feelings about concepts such as heaven and hell, how they view the Bible, and how often they engage in solitary prayer. I would venture to guess that when most people are asked if they are religious, they would think primarily about this intrinsic dimension.

However, that's not the only way to think about how religion intersects with the daily lives of individuals. The extrinsic (or horizontal) dimension recognizes that religion, by and large, is a communal exercise. Every major religious tradition in the world encourages regular corporate worship, and almost all of those sects also emphasize that members should socialize with each other in nonreligious settings as well. For instance in the Christian tradition, communion is celebrated regularly, with a focus on drawing not just closer to God but also to each other. During Ramadan, Muslims come together to break the fast by sharing a meal. Jews who have lost a loved one are encouraged to say the Kaddish prayer as a way to mourn, but this prayer can be said only in the presence of ten other Jews (traditionally men). Religious traditions understand that while intrinsic religiosity is important, it must be supplemented with extrinsic religiosity as well.

Thus, Ruth Benedict's insight that guilt cultures are largely psychological (or vertically oriented), while other cultures are more shame-based and sociological (or horizontal) applies to how we understand religion, as well. These two views of religion tend to cause friction whenever I post a graph on social media with a category for evangelicals who never attend church services. Inevitably, someone will comment that they don't think it's possible to be an evangelical without regularly attending worship. For them, it's impossible to be only a vertically oriented evangelical: religious belief must also be linked with the horizontal dimension (church attendance). But I don't think these never-attending evangelicals are aberrations at all. I think they are actually telling researchers something profoundly important about the way many people perceive religion in the United States.

Many high-attending evangelicals conceive of religion largely in terms of its theological dimension, while ignoring its cultural and political attachments, however. The way I think about the thought process of survey respondents is this. Let's say that I have gone to an evangelical church two or three times in the past five years. When a survey administrator approaches me with a question about my religious tradition, I am faced with a difficult choice. Do I say that I have no religious affiliation? Or do I say that I am an evangelical even though I hardly ever attend? I think that those who report an evangelical affiliation without attending, instead of saying that they are a none, are placing down a marker about how they view themselves in social space. They still see themselves as a person who is religious, even if they don't report any meaningful religious behavior.

Here's how social science conceives of the thought process that someone in that position uses to report their religious affiliation. A person reads the list of religious options and thinks, "Which of these groups represents people like me?" Even though the person doesn't go to church, they aren't necessarily comfortable indicating they have no religious affiliation. They likely have a stereotype in their head of what it means to be religiously unaffiliated—liberal, highly educated, urban—characteristics that don't apply to them that well. On the other hand, they associate the term "evangelical" with blue collar, traditional, conservative folks. For many, this second group sounds more like "people like them," so they indicate they are evangelicals, even if they haven't been to church in years.

How many evangelicals say that they never go to church? And has that changed over time? Figure 8.1 illustrates the findings. About a decade ago, 5 or 6 percent of all people who indicated that they were affiliated with an evangelical religious tradition said that they never attended church services. However, over time that number has begun to slowly creep up. By 2015 or 2016 it was up to 8 percent, and the trend line indicates that about one in ten evangelicals today say that they never show up at a church service. So while never-attenders may still be a small fraction of all evangelicals, that fraction is increasing in size as the years pass.

But what about other aspects of religiosity among those who never attend church services? Are evangelicals who never attend

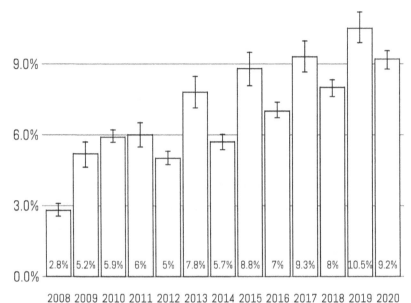

Figure 8.1. Share of Evangelicals Who Never Attend Church

Data from Cooperative Election Study. Stephen Ansolabehere, Brian F. Schaffner, and Sam Luks, Cambridge, MA: Harvard University, http://cces.gov.harvard.edu

church services more likely to say that religion is important in their lives than never-attending Catholics or nones? The answer to the question, as can be seen in figure 8.2, is clearly yes. About 37 percent of evangelicals who never attend church still say that religion is "very important" in their lives. That trails only Black Protestants, half of whom indicate that religion is very important compared to other religious traditions, such as Judaism, of whom only 5.3 percent of never-attenders say religion is very important, or Catholics, of whom just 16 percent say the same. Obviously, atheists and agnostics rank very low on these metrics, with less than 1 percent of each group saying religion is very important.

This pattern appears when the focus is turned to frequency of prayer, as well as in figure 8.3. Both Black Protestants and evangelicals who never attend church are more apt to indicate

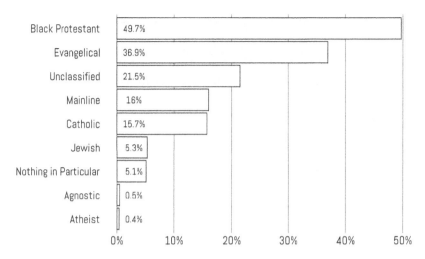

Figure 8.2. Share Saying Religion Is Very Important among Never-Attenders

Data from Cooperative Election Study. Stephen Ansolabehere, Brian F. Schaffner, and Sam Luks, Cambridge, MA: Harvard University, http://cces.gov.harvard.edu

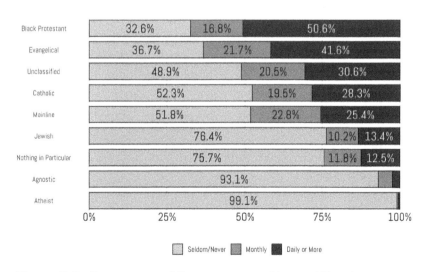

Figure 8.3. Frequency of Prayer among Never-Attenders

Data from Cooperative Election Study. Stephen Ansolabehere, Brian F. Schaffner, and Sam Luks, Cambridge, MA: Harvard University, http://cces.gov.harvard.edu

that they pray at least once a day than they are to report that they never or seldom pray. Among Catholics and mainline Protestants, half report that they pray seldom or never, and three-quarters of Jewish respondents who never attend seldom or never pray. Obviously, huge majorities of atheists and agnostics seldom or never pray, but it's notable that only 93 percent of agnostics report low prayer frequency, while 99 percent of atheists do.

I remember in the church I grew up in hearing at least once a year, "You cannot be a lone ranger Christian." The point that the pastor or Sunday school teacher was trying to make is that religion is, at its essence, a community exercise. I also remember that one preacher compared a Christian who never goes to church to a cell phone that was getting farther away from its data tower. The further a Christian gets away from the church (and other Christians), the more their signal degrades and the less useful their cell phone becomes. Thus, the not-so-subtle message here was that to be a "real" evangelical was to be in the pew every Sunday.

However, that message seems to not land as well for many Americans now as it used to just a decade ago. The share of evangelicals who indicate that they never attend church has continued to rise, despite rhetoric by evangelical leaders to the contrary. But that's not to say that those never-attending evangelicals are not religiously active. The data is clear on this: over 40 percent say that they still pray every day, and nearly the same share report that religion is "very important" in their lives. While many describe these people as "not really evangelicals" because of their lack of church attendance, they are just evangelical in a way that is often not emphasized in these churches. So while many prominent Christian leaders want to construct a view of evangelicals that is predicated on church attendance, there's ample evidence that significant numbers of Americans see evangelicalism as being something broader than just going to a church service.

To return to the guilt-versus-shame framework first proposed by Ruth Benedict, it seems many Americans use a mixture of both approaches when answering questions about their religious beliefs, behaviors, and affiliations. Many never-attending evangelicals seem to be using a guilt-based approach toward their faith. They still identify as evangelical because they believe religion is very important in their lives and they pray frequently—both practices that tap more into the vertical orientation of religion. For this group, church attendance does not make an evangelical. What factors are at play, though, for those who identify as an evangelical yet don't pray, attend church, or place religion at the center of lives? Politics seems to be the most likely culprit.

As can been seen in figure 8.4, the share of never-attending evangelicals who identified as Republicans in 2008 was about

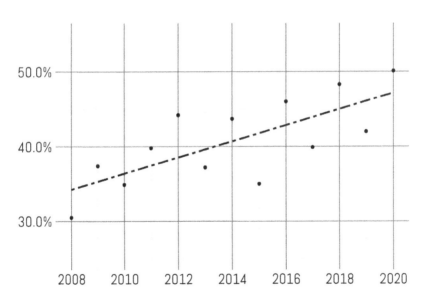

Figure 8.4. Share of Never-Attending Evangelicals Who Identify as Republicans

Data from Cooperative Election Study. Stephen Ansolabehere, Brian F. Schaffner, and Sam Luks, Cambridge, MA: Harvard University, http://cces.gov.harvard.edu

34 percent. In 2020, the share of never-attending evangelicals who aligned with the GOP had jumped to nearly 47 percent—an increase of thirteen percentage points in just twelve years. Recall that in Benedict's understanding, people in shame culture base their identity on how other people view them. For such people, aligning with people who share political beliefs is key to creating a cohesive self-image. The fact that half of never-attending evangelicals are Republicans today, when only 30 percent said the same in 2008, is compelling evidence of an increasing number of Americans understanding that evangelicalism represents not just a theological position but also a political orientation. Thus, when people are asked a question about religious tradition, Republicans implicitly understand that evangelicals share their political viewpoint and check the box next to evangelicalism, despite the fact that they never attend Sunday service.

CONCLUSIONS

There are multiple avenues by which someone might arrive at declaring an evangelical affiliation on a survey. I used to believe that the best approach to measuring American religion was for survey subjects to respond to several questions about religiosity and then researchers should use their answers to place them into religious categories. The rationale behind this approach is that many Americans do not possess a high level of religious literacy; thus, social scientists need to intervene to classify them properly. However, I have changed my approach in recent years. More and more, I am becoming convinced that the best way to find out if someone is an evangelical, or an atheist, or a Latter-day Saint is to just ask them. As Maya Angelou once wrote, "When someone shows you who they are, believe them the first time."

It's not the place of a theologian, a pastor, or a social scientist to tell someone who identifies as evangelical that they don't belong in that religious category. While academics used to believe that someone who identified as evangelical but reported never going to church was merely a survey error, there is mounting evidence now that, on balance, this isn't the case. The way that scholars and religious leaders view matters of faith is not the same as the average American. And, that's okay. When someone reports on a survey that they are an evangelical who never darkens a church door, they are telling us something profoundly important and often too easily dismissed: the way the average person relates to a religious concept is often at odds with the way religious leaders think about that same idea. But that doesn't make one group wrong and the other one right. Instead, it's much more useful for me to believe that everyone expresses their religious faith differently, and it's my job to understand how and why.

For Further Reading

Achen, Christopher H., and Larry M. Bartels. *Democracy for Realists: Why Elections Do Not Produce Responsive Government.* Princeton University Press, 2017.

> While this book may be only tangentially related to the study of religion and politics, it's one of the most important works I've read in the past five years. Achen and Bartels' discussion of how voters place themselves in social and political spaces reshaped the way that I think about the role religion plays in the lives of Americans and got me interested in studying the phenomenon of evangelicals who don't go to church.

Burge, Ryan. "Are We All Evangelicals Now? How the Term Has Grown to Blur Theology and Ideology," *Religion Unplugged,*

March 11, 2021, https://religionunplugged.com/news/ 2021/3/11/are-we-all-evangelicals-now-how-the-term-has- grown-to-blur-theology-and-ideology.

Adjacent to the topic covered in this chapter is another intriguing question: Can someone be an evangelical if they don't identify as a Protestant? The data indicates they absolutely can be. In fact, there are increasing numbers of evangelical Jews, Muslims, and Orthodox Christians. It appears evangelical has come to denote theological conservatism and religious devotion.

Zaller, John R. *The Nature and Origins of Mass Opinion*. Cambridge University Press, 1992.

This is a very technical and academic work, but it has tremendous implications for how we should think about polling. Zaller contends that when we ask questions on surveys, the responses we get are often the first thing that comes to mind for most respondents. Thus, we need to be careful about how we ask questions and the order in which we ask them. This is especially true when polling about religion.

The personal faith of a presidential candidate can activate part of the electorate

THE FALL 2020 SCHOOL TERM WAS ALREADY SHAP-
ing up to be an incredibly busy semester, but something else
was going on that diverted my attention from advising students,
planning courses, and organizing a small conference: the 2020
presidential election.

Every news outlet in the United States and across the world
was trying to find a new way to spin the same old horse race–style
coverage of presidential elections. No one wants to read the same
basic story from five or six different media outlets that all cover
the same details in a similar fashion. So editors tell reporters,
"Find a new angle on this" and they begin to scour the internet
and talk to sources in hopes of finding another way to frame the
November contest. Apparently, some of them managed to zero
in on the impact religion would have on the presidential vote,
because my inbox began pinging in early October and continued
through Thanksgiving with requests for interviews, data points,
and musings about how the matchup between Joe Biden and
Donald Trump played out among the faithful going to the polls.

Many of the questions I received from reporters were focused
on the personal faith of the Democratic nominee, Joe Biden.
Biden had never shied away from speaking about his Catholic

upbringing, both as a member of the United States Senate and as the Vice-President. However, pictures of Biden coming or going from Mass while on the campaign trail became a steady part of the media coverage of his candidacy in 2020. Having seen those images and heard the chatter on social media, lots of political analysts thought this would give Biden the ability to win over larger shares of the Catholic vote than Hillary Clinton received in 2016. However, when I was asked by reporters if I thought Biden would be well positioned to take a larger share of the Catholic vote, I couldn't provide the full-throated support for the theory that they wanted. There's very little evidence that any candidate in the past several decades has been especially adept at winning over certain religious groups.

But data availability and quality issues aside, there's another more existential problem with the media coverage around election season: in most cases, the vote choice among faith groups does not shift in any meaningful way from one presidential election to the next. Journalists are always hunting for the big headline, like "White Evangelicals vote share for Donald Trump dropped by ten points in his reelection bid" or "Why did atheists support Biden in much larger numbers than they did Clinton four years earlier?" Unfortunately, the data indicates almost no sweeping changes happen at the intersection of religion and politics every four years. Instead, most of the movement in the electorate is much more incremental. A one- or two-point shift between two elections can become an eight-point swing across four election cycles.

Looking across data from presidential elections from 2008 through 2020 in figure 9.1 makes it clear how these trends develop with some groups over time. For instance, only 3 percent of Black Protestants voted for John McCain in 2008. Mitt Romney did two points better, then Donald Trump got 7 percent in 2016 and 9 percent in 2020. That same gradual trend appears for Orthodox Christians, Buddhists, and Hindus as well. But generally, most of

Figure 9.1. Vote Share for the Republican Presidential Candidate (2008–2020)

Data from Cooperative Election Study. Stephen Ansolabehere, Brian F. Schaffner, and Sam Luks, Cambridge, MA: Harvard University, http://cces.gov.harvard.edu

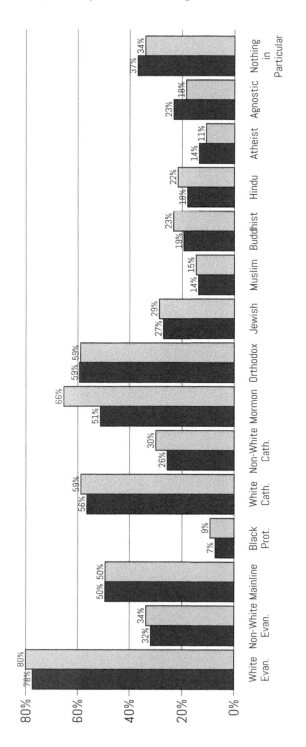

Figure 9.2. Vote Share for Trump in 2016 vs. 2020

Data from Cooperative Election Study. Stephen Ansolabehere, Brian F. Schaffner, and Sam Luks, Cambridge, MA: Harvard University, http://cces.gov.harvard.edu

the trend lines are relatively flat over four election cycles. Stability among religious groups at the voting booth is very much the expected outcome.

The results from the 2016 and 2020 presidential elections illustrate this point very well in figure 9.2. What makes the 2020 election a bit different from the 2016 contest is that there was an incumbent—President Trump was vying for a second term in office. When only one of the two candidates changes in an election, the likelihood of dramatic shifts in the way that electorate votes is fairly low. The other notable aspect of the 2020 election was that Donald Trump had seen no significant shifts in his approval rating across his four years in the White House. Thus, there was not a lot of reason to believe that the forty-fifth president had either turned off a big portion of his base or that he had won over independents or conservative Democrats between 2016 and 2020.

The data bears that out pretty clearly. Most religious groups shifted just a few percentage points between the two races. For instance, the overall shift in vote share for Donald Trump among evangelicals was only two percentage points in his favor. Among mainline Protestants, there was absolutely no change. For Catholics, the shift was slightly larger than it was for evangelicals at just about three percentage points overall. Among the smaller religious groups such as Muslims, Buddhists, Hindus, and Jews, the movement was two or three percentage points in Trump's direction as well. Among the religiously unaffiliated, Trump lost about four percentage points of support in his reelection bid. But read those numbers again: the overall shift among any religious group never exceeds four percentage points. That's not what I would describe as a large swing.

Really, the only religious group that shifted significantly between the 2016 and 2020 presidential elections was the Latter-day Saints vote. In 2016, Trump got a very slim majority of the LDS vote, but that's not because Hillary Clinton was seen as a particularly attractive candidate to the LDS community. Rather, they didn't particularly like either of the two major party candidates. Instead, nearly a quarter of the LDS vote went to third-party candidates, with many casting a ballot for Evan McMullin (a moderate Republican who is a member of the LDS church). Because neither McMullin nor any other viable third-party candidates ran in 2020, the LDS voters had to decide between Trump and Biden; thus, both parties did better with LDS voters in 2020. Or, in short, the LDS vote was truly an outlier.

But what happens if we pull back the time frame and compare the election results from the 2020 presidential election to the matchup of Barack Obama and John McCain back in November 2008? Remember, that election was by any objective viewpoint a blowout for Barack Obama. Obama beat John McCain by over seven percentage points in the popular vote but also won states that seemed far out of reach for any Democratic candidate running in 2020. So if we were looking for big shifts in vote share, it should be through comparing 2008 to any subsequent election.

But if the results from 2008 and 2020 are visualized for all the religious traditions in figure 9.3, the changes are not nearly as dramatic as many would anticipate (or the media would hope for). For most of the largest religious traditions in the United States, the actual shift in the overall vote was relatively minor over those twelve years. Take many of the largest Christian traditions, for instance. Despite all the think pieces written about how Donald Trump would turn off white evangelicals in both 2016 and 2020, he actually did better than John McCain did—but by only three percentage points. The same three-point shift to the Republican side is evident among white Catholics as well. Among mainline, the movement is just two percentage points, also the case among non-white Catholics and Protestants.

In fact, if you are looking for big swings, there are only four religious groups whose vote share for Donald Trump was at least

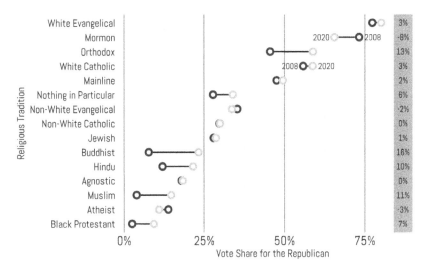

Figure 9.3. Change in Republican Vote Share from 2008 to 2020

Data from Cooperative Election Study. Stephen Ansolabehere, Brian F. Schaffner, and Sam Luks, Cambridge, MA: Harvard University, http://cces.gov.harvard.edu

ten points different from what it was for John McCain. Those four groups were: Orthodox Christians, Buddhists, Hindus, and Muslims. But in total those four groups constitute about 2.5 percent of the adult population of the United States. So while there were significant swings in the vote share of some religious groups, they represent a very small fraction of the total votes cast. Among these four groups, their vote share switching resulted in the changing of one in four hundred votes cast on election day—clearly, not enough to make the difference in who wins the White House. For comparison, getting 1 percent of the white evangelical vote to switch to the Democrat would net more overall votes than getting 10 percent of Hindus, Muslims, Buddhists, and Orthodox Christians to change their votes.

I think the reason the media anticipate tectonic shifts in the vote of religious groups is that observers focus in general on each presidential candidate's unique strengths and weaknesses, assuming these particular characteristics will help them win over new voters—while acknowledging, if they're honest, that these same traits could hurt their chances with other demographic segments of the electorate. For instance, when Barack Obama ran for president in 2008, one of the easiest ways to attack his candidacy was that he lacked experience. That was undoubtedly the case, as he had served only two years in the United States Senate before declaring his candidacy for the highest office in the land. The Obama team tried to counter this by talking about that lack of experience as an advantage. Recall all the discussion about "hope" and "change" during the 2008 campaign.

In the same way, candidates themselves (and their campaign advisors, of course) focus on their religious background, believing this aspect of their biography will have significant influence on voters' choices. George W. Bush had a very strong following among evangelical Protestants, because he saw himself as an evangelical and was conversant in the terminology and culture of that strain of American Christianity. Bush made it a point to talk about how his born-again experience helped him end his alcohol addiction and become a better husband and father. In much the same way, Joe Biden did not shy away from talking about his strong commitment to the Roman Catholic Church while on the campaign trail. That was a sharp contrast to the prior Democratic nominee, Hillary Clinton, who was a lifelong United Methodist but did not emphasize that during her run for the White House. Given these differing strategies, one might assume Biden was well positioned to win over a bigger share of the white Catholic vote in 2020 than Clinton received just four years earlier.

However, if we dig into the data about presidential vote choice among white Catholics in 2016 and 2020, we find no evidence in

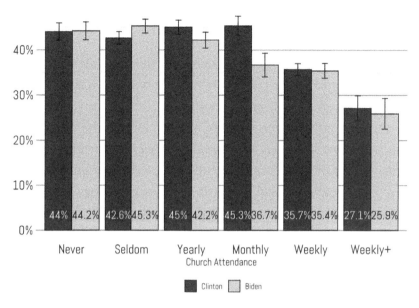

Figure 9.4. Vote Share for the Democrat in 2016 vs. 2020 among White Catholics

Data from Cooperative Election Study. Stephen Ansolabehere, Brian F. Schaffner, and Sam Luks, Cambridge, MA: Harvard University, http://cces.gov.harvard.edu

figure 9.4 that Biden won any more of this voting bloc than Clinton did. If the white Catholic vote is subdivided into levels of church attendance, Biden did not do significantly better than Clinton in a single attendance category. In fact, in five of the six categories there were no statistically significant differences between the two election cycles. Among monthly attending white Catholics, Hillary Clinton earned 45 percent of the vote in 2016, but Joe Biden actually did eight points worse four years later. If you had handpicked a candidate primarily to gain back the white Catholic voting bloc in the 2020 presidential election, it would have been hard to find a more ideal person than Joe Biden. But Biden's share of the white Catholic vote in 2020 was not statistically distinct from Clinton's share four years earlier.

CONCLUSIONS

It's fair to say that the media latches on to candidates and likes to tell a compelling narrative about their backstory, their ability to attract new voters, and how they will compete with others in the field to gain the votes of swing blocs of the electorate. But in almost all cases, the reasons for victory (or defeat) in a presidential election are not really about the candidate or the campaign at all. Political scientists have been writing for decades about the idea that a campaign is not really that consequential to the outcome of the race—what's called the minimal effects hypothesis. At its core, proponents of this view argue that the candidates and their campaigns have a very small impact on the overall outcome of presidential races. Things like debates, conventions, and gaffes are little more than fodder for the talking heads on television to debate endlessly. Like the characteristics of the candidates themselves, the vast majority of these campaign-related events have a small and short-lived impact on the vote choice of Americans.

This hypothesis argues that most elections are decided long before the parties select their nominees. A question such as "Is there an incumbent president?" is orders of magnitude more important than how often a nominee goes to church. That's because those who study political science know with a high degree of certainty that a reasonably popular incumbent is nearly impossible to beat in a reelection campaign. And if there's not an incumbent president, then other factors take on great significance, none more than the state of the economy. A recession is going to hurt the party that is in power, as it undoubtedly did John McCain in 2008. President Bush was largely blamed for allowing the Great Recession to begin, but McCain, as the Republican party's nominee, had to shoulder that negative sentiment as well. No matter what voters thought of him personally—how well he debated or how slick his convention speech was—he couldn't overcome skyrocketing unemployment and a frozen credit market.

The last thing I want to do is write myself out of my job, but in the phrase "religion and politics," it seems that politics is more important than ever before. The idea that large swaths of Americans are willing to listen honestly and openly to the arguments from both sides of the political spectrum is more a product of wishful thinking than statistical reality. And, it's also idealistic to think that voters place their religious affiliation at the center of the political decision-making process. Instead, the vast majority of political scientists contend that partisanship is the most important factor in the lives of most Americans, with faith a distant second. If that's how most voters make their decision on election day, then it's inevitable that religious voting blocs won't shift significantly from one election to the next—no matter how compelling the candidate.

For Further Reading

Berelson, Bernard R., Paul F. Lazarsfeld, and William N. McPhee. *Voting: A Study of Opinion Formation in a Presidential Campaign*. University of Chicago Press, 1986.

Using the town of New Haven, Connecticut, as their research lab, a team of political scientists at Yale University sets out to understand how people make decisions about who to vote for on election day. In the process they wrote one of the seminal works on political behavior. The scholars concluded that vote choices are influenced largely by social concerns and that the impact of friends, family, and religious institutions are key factors in understanding political behavior.

Campbell, Angus, Philip E. Converse, Warren E. Miller, and Donald E. Stokes. *The American Voter*. University of Chicago Press, 1980.

One of the most foundational works in American voting behavior is *The American Voter*, which was written by a team of scholars at the University of Michigan. They argue that there is no stronger factor in American voting behavior than party identification. They contend that voters create a psychological attachment to a certain party, and all information is then funneled through that worldview. This makes it nearly impossible for people to change their minds about their vote choice.

Hillygus, D. Sunshine, and Simon Jackman. "Voter Decision Making in Election 2000: Campaign Effects, Partisan Activation, and the Clinton Legacy." *American Journal of Political Science* 47, no. 4 (2003): 583–96.

Setting out to directly test the minimal effects hypothesis, Hillygus and Jackman conducted a regular survey of the same sample over the last several months of the 2000 presidential campaign. This allowed them to understand when voters made up their minds about how to cast their ballot and what events directly preceded those changes. Generally, they found that campaign events really mattered only for true political independents and undecided voters.

People return to religion late in life

I HAVE PASTORED TWO CHURCHES IN MY ADULT LIFE. Both were in rural Illinois and affiliated with the American Baptist denomination. Both had a very long history in their community with many influential leaders in the area claiming membership at one point or another. When I began to serve each of them, they were by any objective definition very small congregations. An average Sunday's group of worshippers would have fit into a typical high school classroom. But the characteristic that seemed to loom over every decision we made in both congregations was that our assemblies featured a lot of gray hair and a huge percentage of the faithful living on Social Security, a pension, or retirement savings. To put it even more bluntly, the members of both churches were really old: the average age was easily seventy when I took over the job.

I took the pastorate at the first church when I had just turned twenty-three and assumed the pulpit of my current calling before my twenty-fifth birthday. It's not an exaggeration to say that I was the youngest person in the sanctuary on most Sundays by at least three decades. That obviously took some getting used to in the first few years. Lots of pastors try to seem relevant by sprinkling in pop culture references throughout their sermons, but those strategies don't have the desired effect when most of your congregation's idea of good music is Lawrence Welk and their favorite movie is *Gone with the Wind*. It was a bumpy road for a while: a young unmarried man, trying to relate to a group of folks who had grandchildren my age. But as time passed, we warmed up to each other. What really helped cement my place with my current church is that I got married and had two children. I am only partially joking when I say that my boys have about six sets of grandparents, but only some of them are related to them by blood.

When someone asks me about my current congregation, I try to quickly mention our size, the shrinking numbers of people in the pews, and the fact that most of our faithful members were born before World War II. Many of them shake their heads in amazement and ask, in a very sincere tone, "How do you make that work?" Which, I admit, is a really hard question to answer. I try to explain that even though we come from vastly different generations and life experiences, at our core all people are the same. We value friendship, community, a sense of belonging, and a need to find meaning in our everyday lives. Our church, and thousands like us, are built on those things that we hold in common. Many of them still don't seem entirely convinced that an arrangement like ours can work, but many times they will end the conversation by making a statement such as, "It does make sense that older people are the ones coming to church; it's almost like they are cramming for the final exam."

The sentiment is one I think many people share—that people may drift from religion during their youth or even through middle age, but when their children move out of the house, they retire from their jobs, and things slow down, they start contemplating their own mortality. The old saying, "There are no atheists in a foxhole," could easily be modified: "There are no atheists in a retirement community." People assume when they look at a congregation like mine that many of the folks who show up on Sunday morning weren't faithful attenders until later in life—that the older members who make up a large proportion of many churches' membership rolls are returnees. But the statistical reality doesn't bear that out. Instead, what is really happening is that as people age, they are actually less likely to go church than when they were younger. And that trend has only accelerated in the past decade.

Before we get to the data, it seems helpful to describe how social scientists think about the way religiosity changes as one goes through all the ages. I think we can all admit that the child our parents raised is not the same person who is reading this book right now. And, it's also fair to say that many of us look back on the irresponsible things we did in our late teens and early twenties and are amazed we made it out alive. For most people, religion fades in importance during these crucial formative years, and then it takes on an entirely different role as we move into adulthood, get married, have children, and start settling down. How this all relates to religion is often termed the *life cycle effect*, illustrated in figure 10.1.

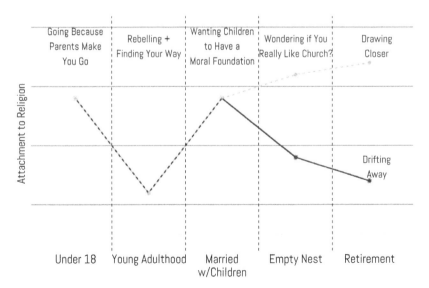

Figure 10.1. Visualizing the Life Cycle Effect

Most young people don't have much agency when it comes to religion. They go to church because their parents make them. Yes, many children and teenagers do enjoy the socialization and camaraderie of the youth group experience. But it's fair to say that many young people form a stronger attachment to a religious community because of the implicit (or explicit) encouragement of parents to go to church camp and lock-ins than they would have without that parental nudge. Then those children turn eighteen years old, graduate from high school, and, in many cases, move away from home. Even those who decide not to further their education will more than likely begin to loosen ties with their parents and exert some level of independence in young adulthood.

What tends to happen for many of them is that they drift away from religion. For a good portion, though, this path is more a function of logistics than spirituality. Moving to a new town is hard enough, but also having to figure out how to budget, do laundry, manage your time, and stay out of trouble is a tall order for many eighteen-year-olds who have constantly lived under the supervision of parents. Finding a new church in a college town is fraught with pitfalls. Many young people are comfortable with the kind of Christianity they grew up with, but to find a close copy of that in a college town can be really difficult. The result is that many stop going altogether, and this lack of churchgoing extends for many of them into their mid to late twenties as they search for career stability, often moving in search of employment and generally living in a constant state of flux.

However, as many people move into their late twenties and early thirties, things begin to slow down a little bit, and the basic framework of an adult life begins to emerge. Most young people begin to settle into a long-term career field, decide where they want to live for the next several years, and find a spouse. They may begin to have children. All these milestones can lead people to reconnect with their religious upbringing. Lots of couples will contact a minister or priest to conduct their nuptials and hold their ceremony in a sanctuary. Then, when children come, many traditions have infant baptism or christening ceremonies that also provide opportunities for a return to religion.

As those children grow, parents tend to want to raise their offspring with the same moral foundation they had when they were kids, so they get back into the habit of churchgoing. Attending vacation Bible schools and Sunday school classes soon transitions into teenagers becoming part of the youth group. Many times the parents also increase their attachment to the churches, as it seems like the natural thing to do. But then, those children grow up, graduate from high school, and leave home. What are parents to do at this point? That's where the life cycle effect is less precise. Many empty nesters become even more attached to their religious community as a way to keep strong social ties and a sense of purpose. Others begin to realize they were going to church only because their children did and drift away from religious attachment.

It's hard to compare the religiosity of a group like empty nesters today with that same portion of the population even a decade ago. The primary reason is that the religious makeup of American society has shifted fairly significantly in just the past ten years. In 2008, just over 22 percent of the population had no religious affiliation, but by 2020 that had jumped to 34 percent. Thus, we should expect that a larger share of people in their fifties or sixties would have no religious affiliation in 2020 compared to 2008 just by virtue of increased secularization in society as a whole. So comparing the religiosity of a fifty-five-year-old in 2008 to that of a fifty-five-year-old in 2020 is not the most helpful comparison.

Instead, the best way to analyze how people are shifting their religious belonging as they move through the life-cycle effect is via birth cohort analysis, which is to break the sample into groups based on the year of their birth. Typically, this is done in five-year birth cohorts, and by analyzing these birth cohorts over a longer period of time, we are able to draw conclusions about how people who went through life experiencing similar things at the same point in their lives changed their behavior based on what was going on in society at large. The CES makes this a viable method, because the sheer sample size of each birth cohort affords us the ability to track even relatively small changes over a long period of time. In this case, we want to track religious disaffiliation.

The oldest birth cohort that can be analyzed were those born between 1930 and 1934, which means this group was in their seventies when first contacted by the CES in the first wave of the survey in 2008. The youngest cohort was those born between 1995 and 2000, and because this is only a survey of adults, they were not part of the sample until 2013 and thus can be tracked only from that point forward. However, what's valuable is that between the oldest and youngest cohorts we are able to gauge how people at all stages of life are claiming no religious affiliation between 2008 and 2020.

For instance, those in the top row of figure 10.2 represent people who were either retired or very close to retirement age when they took part in the survey. For many in this group, life was stable. They did not have to worry about finding a job, their children were raised and out of the house, and most were living off retirement income and savings. As the life cycle effect would predict, there's not a great deal of shifting in their overall level of religiosity. However, that's not to say this group has been immune to secularization. In fact, for those born 1940–44 and 1945–49, the rate of religious disaffiliation increased six and seven percentage points, respectively, between 2008 and 2020. These are people who are moving rapidly toward the end of their lives, yet there's no real evidence of "cramming for the final exam"—just the opposite, in fact.

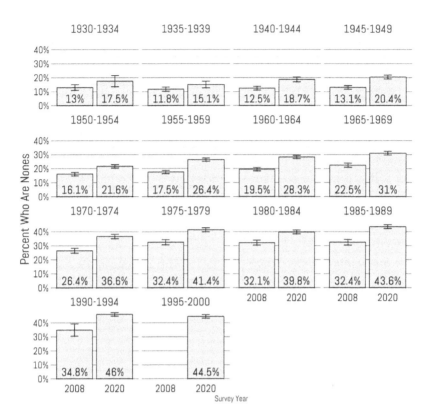

Figure 10.2. Cohort Analysis of Religious Disaffiliation from 2008 to 2020

Data from Cooperative Election Study. Stephen Ansolabehere, Brian F. Schaffner, and Sam Luks, Cambridge, MA: Harvard University, http://cces.gov.harvard.edu

However, the oldest Americans are following the same trend as the rest of the US population. Among these birth cohorts, the ones most likely to become empty nesters between 2008 and 2020 were those born in the 1960s and 1970s. As previously discussed, this is the time when many people begin to reassess the need for church in their lives. Well, the evidence seems to indicate that when their children leave home and go off on their own, larger shares of their parents realize they don't want to be attached to religion. The rate of disaffiliation for these birth cohorts increased from 8.5 to 10 percent between 2008 and 2020. Thus, there's really no evidence here that people return to religion as they move into the latter stages of life.

In fact, there's no evidence of any birth cohort returning to religion between 2008 and 2020. Recall that the life cycle effect predicts that as people move into their late twenties and thirties, they are more likely to find their way back to faith. That's just not reflected in these results. Among those born in 1985 or later, there should be evidence of disaffiliation reversing or at least abating, as many in these cohorts were moving into solid careers and families in the time period under study. Yet disaffiliation shot up over eleven percentage points for those born between 1985 and 1994. Even here, there's no reason to believe that religious affiliation vacillates up and down. The line points in only one direction and that's upward.

CONCLUSIONS

One of my favorite classes to teach is research methods. The goal of that course is for students to begin to think about the world in a rigorously empirical way. What that means in a practical sense is that they become aware of the myriad of ways in which research studies can be flawed and also how our own personal thinking can be clouded by emotion or cognitive bias. Trying to see our own blind spots is one of the most difficult tasks that social scientists have to grapple with when writing a manuscript for publication. I also feel the same way when I try to put together a Sunday sermon and can see only one interpretation of a biblical text. We all know we are missing something in our research design, theoretical construction, or data analysis, but we can never be entirely sure what the missing piece is until we send it off for review.

All of us make those same sorts of mistakes in our own daily lives. We are constantly taking in information and quickly analyzing it. Many of us just don't have the inclination, time, and mental energy it takes to constantly reevaluate the way we view the world. So when we constantly see pictures or video of church services filled with lots of old people, we just naturally assume that's because people come back toward religion as they age. Unfortunately, this is a perfect example of a concept called survivorship bias.

Let me illustrate with one of my favorite stories in social science. In World War II, the United States used air power at a large scale for the first time in a theater of war. Because it was an entirely new way to fight, the military was focused on learning from their mistakes, so that they could keep planes in the air longer and minimize the death of Army Air Force pilots. To do that, servicemen would rigorously examine the aircraft that had returned from bombing missions looking for bullet holes. They would carefully map where the highest concentrations of bullets had hit the planes and use that data to reinforce those areas in the next round of planes that were rolling off the assembly line.

But there's one major problem with that research design: the servicemen couldn't examine the planes that had been shot down over the battlefield and never returned to the hangar. Wouldn't it be a bit more useful for Air Force mechanics to know where the enemy was shooting the planes that actually caused them to crash? By reinforcing the areas that were full of bullet holes among the planes that did make it back safely, they were protecting areas that were not at all critical to the operation of the aircraft. That's what survivorship bias is—our tendency to think about the things that we do see and to ignore the things that we do not.

In our specific instance, we see pews full of people with gray hair and assume that this is the result of people returning to church as they age—a classic case of survivorship bias. Instead, what is really happening is that almost all of those people who identify as Christian now would have identified as Christians when they were in their twenties or forties. They did not return to faith—they never left, and that's impossible to perceive unless you've been part of the church for decades. The data tells us the clearest story: secularization is happening to every birth cohort dating back to the 1940s.

For Further Reading

Margolis, Michele F. *From Politics to the Pews*. University of Chicago Press, 2018.

> In this very important book, Margolis examines the relationship between politics and religion as individuals age. She concludes that people more frequently choose their church based on political considerations, not theological positions. This obviously has tremendous implications for the future of American society.

The State of Pastors. Barna Research Group, 2017.

> While this chapter focuses on the age of those in the pews, we would be remiss to forget about those leading the weekend worship service. In conjunction with Pepperdine University, the Barna Research Group conducted a survey of American pastors and found that while just a quarter of pastors were 55 or older in 1992, that had increased to half by 2017.

Stolzenberg, Ross M., Mary Blair-Loy, and Linda J. Waite. "Religious Participation in Early Adulthood: Age and Family Life

Cycle Effects on Church Membership." *American Sociological Review* (1995): 84–103.

If you are interested in how religiosity shifts as we age, this article is a good place to begin. The authors find that a variety of factors, such as divorce, cohabitation, and the age of parents, impact church attendance. However, it's important to note that this discussion is based on data from the 1970s and 1980s, when the share of Americans who were secular was not very large.

Abortion is the most important issue for evangelical voters

IN 2017, THE STATE OF ALABAMA CONVENED A SPEcial election to fill the Senate seat vacated by Jeff Sessions when he was confirmed as the Attorney General of the United States. Initially the Alabama contest was seen by many as a referendum on the presidency of Donald Trump. However, the focus of the race quickly changed from national issues to the two candidates.

The Alabama Democrats had nominated Doug Jones, a moderate who had a long history of political activism in the state. The Republicans had chosen Roy Moore, who had been removed as the Chief Justice of the Alabama Supreme Court for refusing to take down a monument to the Ten Commandments from the rotunda of the Supreme Court building in Montgomery. In the days before the special election, the *Washington Post* published a story centering around a woman who alleged that Roy Moore tried to initiate a sexual encounter with her when she was fourteen years old and he was thirty-two.[19]

The belief that the race in Alabama was really about Donald Trump began to fade as more women came forward accusing Moore of sexually inappropriate behavior. The issues facing Republicans in Alabama crystallized when the *Los Angeles Times* interviewed a voter named Ellen Tipton about her decision in the upcoming election. Tipton noted that Moore was "an embarrassment to

Alabama." But then she expounded, "I just can't believe we're down to this. I'm torn between voting for a pedophile and voting for a person who believes in abortion."[20]

Thus, in just a few words, Ellen Tipton encapsulated one of the most pervasive myths in American religion and politics—that many evangelical voters in the United States back the GOP because they cannot stomach voting for a candidate or a party that defends a woman's right to have an abortion. The sentiment is so deeply embedded in the public consciousness that when I have tried to challenge that assumption, I've had more than one person scoff and refuse to hear the rest of my argument. But both history and survey data indicate that the alliance between evangelicals and pro-life views is not nearly as strong as many people believe them to be.

A quick perusal of some of the writings of evangelical publications in the 1960s indicates that the prevailing notion prior to Roe v. Wade (decided in 1973) was that abortion was not a desirable outcome, but it certainly wasn't considered an unqualified evil (as it is today by many evangelicals). For instance, a 1971 resolution passed by the messengers at the Southern Baptist Convention encouraged "legislation that will allow the possibility of abortion under such conditions as rape, incest, clear evidence of severe fetal deformity, and carefully ascertained evidence of the likelihood of damage to the emotional, mental, and physical health of the mother."[21] That same resolution was affirmed in both 1974[22] and 1976,[23] as well.

How did the views of many evangelicals begin to shift on the topic of abortion? Ample evidence provided by Randall Balmer in his 2006 book, *Thy Kingdom Come*,[24] indicates that many leaders of the Religious Right in the 1980s and 1990s viewed abortion as an ideal issue to activate the base of evangelicals, who generally preferred Republican candidates but were not very motivated to go to the polls or attend rallies. Men like Paul Weyrich and Jerry

Falwell believed the issue of abortion was well situated to get out the vote for the GOP because of its visceral and emotional nature. They knew, for example, that the millions of evangelicals who for decades had been tepid about political engagement would have a hard time ignoring graphic images of aborted fetuses.

This close relationship between evangelicals and the Republican party was described in great detail in Thomas Frank's *What's the Matter with Kansas?*, published in 2004.[25] Frank centers his narrative around his own personal story of being raised in a Kansas that was decidedly not politically conservative but then returning as an adult to find a state that was deep red in its political orientation. Frank argues that the Republican Party convinced many poor Christians in states like Kansas to vote against their economic self-interests by pushing issues like abortion to the center of the American political debate. To Frank, what happened in Kansas was that Republican politicians convinced poor evangelicals to vote for the GOP so abortion would be banned. But once Republicans won majorities in the legislature, their policies focused on deregulation and tax cuts for the wealthy, while making no significant headway on abortion. Despite the fact that empirical political science has largely debunked the notion that many evangelicals vote against their own economic interests (something I address in myth 12), Frank's argument put down deep roots in the American understanding of religion and politics.

But I've dug into the data on this topic from a variety of angles, using a number of statistical tools, and I find the image of the single-issue white evangelical voter has no real basis in any type of statistical reality. However, I also find fairly compelling evidence that abortion is not the single issue that is driving the votes of white evangelicals. Instead, there's evidence that immigration is just as important an issue as abortion.

In 2016, the Cooperative Election Study included a fascinating battery of questions that asked respondents to indicate how

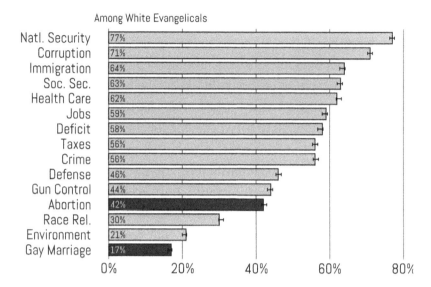

Figure 11.1. Share Saying Issue Is of Very High Importance among White Evangelicals

Data from Cooperative Election Study. Stephen Ansolabehere, Brian F. Schaffner, and Sam Luks, Cambridge, MA: Harvard University, http://cces.gov.harvard.edu

important fifteen issues were to them with response options ranging from "no importance at all" to "very high importance." Topics included national security, gun control, immigration, health care, jobs, as well as two classic culture war issues: gay marriage and abortion. The share of white evangelicals who indicated they saw each issue as having "very high importance" provides an illuminating picture of this religious voting bloc in figure 11.1.

The issue that leads the way, by a fairly significant margin, is national security. But looking down the list of issues in order of importance, a pattern begins to emerge. The things that the majority of white evangelicals care about could most accurately be described as "bread and butter" conservative politics—things like corruption, jobs, the deficit, and crime. The takeaway seems to be that white evangelicals care about the same things that a stereotypical Republican would care about—a concept that I will talk about in more detail in myth 12.

The bottom of the graph represents the issues that seem to elicit the lowest level of concern among white evangelicals: gun control, abortion, race relations, the environment, and gay marriage. In the case of gun control, race relations, and the environment, it's fairly clear why white evangelicals don't place a high importance on these topics. They don't want gun control, many don't express a great deal of concern about the environment, and (as recent events have shown) many Republicans don't give a great deal of credence to concepts like systemic racism.

But if white evangelicals really care about social issues, it's pretty hard to explain why such small shares of white evangelical voters don't think gay marriage and abortion are that important. Just 42.2 percent of white evangelicals indicate that abortion is of "very high importance"—twenty-five points less than national security and twenty-one points less than immigration. Gay marriage scores even lower, with just 17 percent of white evangelicals believing the issue is of very high importance. In 2004, just twelve years before this poll was conducted, eleven states passed amendments to their constitutions codifying marriage as between one man and one woman. The smallest margin of victory was in the state of Oregon, where 57 percent of voters supported a constitutional ban on same sex marriage.[26] In 2016, only 17 percent of white evangelicals thought same-sex marriage was of very high importance. There's little evidence that social issues are "top of mind" thoughts when white evangelicals go to the polls.

But I want to put this idea to a more strenuous test. There's no doubt that immigration was thrust into the spotlight through the rhetoric and policies of President Donald Trump. Stories about migrant caravans moving up through Central America on their way to the southern border of the United States were regularly

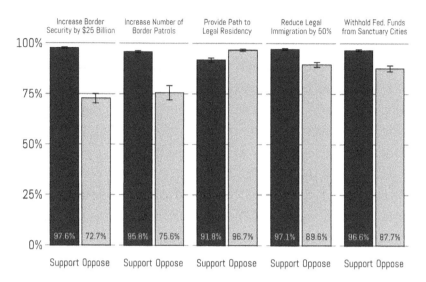

Figure 11.2. Donald Trump Approval among White Evangelical Republicans by Position on Immigration Policy

Data from Cooperative Election Study. Stephen Ansolabehere, Brian F. Schaffner, and Sam Luks, Cambridge, MA: Harvard University, http://cces.gov.harvard.edu

picked up by national media outlets. Trump's legal challenge of DREAM act provisions along with his Muslim travel ban were some of his administration's most high-profile policy changes. It's fair to say that there may have been no more salient policy area between 2016 and 2020 than immigration. But how much did Trump's support depend on his stances on immigration? To test that question, I looked at his approval rating among white evangelical Republicans based on the stances that those individuals had on immigration policy proposals. The results are displayed in figure 11.2.

It's logical that those white evangelical Republicans who hold the same views of immigration policy as Donald Trump would support him at higher levels. In fact, among those white evangelical Republicans who hold more conservative views of immigration, Trump's approval rating never dips below 96 percent.

However, among that same group of white evangelical Republicans, Trump's approval rating is lower among those who don't hold such a conservative view of immigration. For instance, among white evangelical Republicans who don't want to see increased border patrols, his approval rating is 76 percent, and it's only 72 percent among those who don't want to spend more money on border security.

So it's clear that Trump's approval rating among white evangelical Republicans does depend, at least in some part, on his immigration policies. But what about abortion? Are pro-choice white evangelical Republicans more likely to express lower levels of support than pro-immigration white evangelical Republicans? The evidence in figure 11.3 seems to indicate that abortion has less bearing on Trump's approval rating than many people would have guessed.

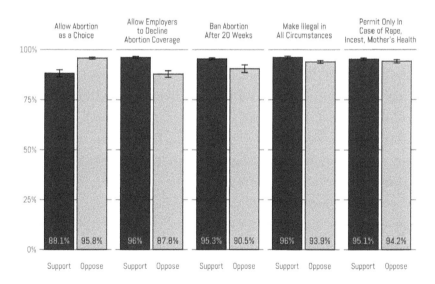

Figure 11.3. Trump Approval among White Evangelical Republicans by Position on Abortion Policy

Data from Cooperative Election Study. Stephen Ansolabehere, Brian F. Schaffner, and Sam Luks, Cambridge, MA: Harvard University, http://cces.gov.harvard.edu

Notice how little difference there is in Trump's approval rating in 2020 between white evangelical Republicans who take a more conservative view of abortion versus those who favor some pro-choice policies. For instance, 96 percent of white evangelical Republicans who oppose a woman's right to choose an abortion approved of Donald Trump, but 88 percent of those who favored a woman's right to choose supported Trump. The gap in approval based on views of a late-term abortion ban was less than five percentage points. And what strikes me as the most telling result is on the question of making abortion illegal in all circumstances. Among white evangelical Republicans who favor a complete ban on all abortions, Trump's approval rating was 96 percent. Among those who don't favor such a ban, 94 percent support him. If ending Roe v. Wade, and outlawing abortion is the key driver of the white evangelical vote, then why does Donald Trump's support depend so little on making abortion illegal?

But I did one last test to really understand the reasons for Trump's approval among white evangelical Republicans. I divided white evangelical Republicans into four groups based on how they answered the question about a woman's right to choose and their support of reducing legal immigration to the United States by 50 percent. I then constructed a regression model, so I could control for a variety of other factors—such as church attendance, age, education, income, and gender—that could possibly explain Trump's support. By including these other variables, it's possible to say, holding these demographic factors constant, *here* is the impact of abortion and immigration policy on Trump's approval rating. The results of this model are visualized in figure 11.4.

Unsurprisingly, the group that indicates the highest level of support for Donald Trump was white evangelical Republicans who were pro-life and anti-immigration, and those who supported him the least were those who were pro-choice and pro-immigration. But the other two groups tell an interesting story about the policy

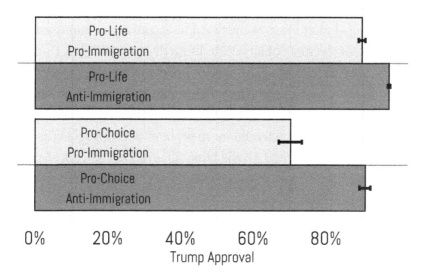

Figure 11.4. Trump Approval among White Evangelical Republicans

Data from Cooperative Election Study. Stephen Ansolabehere, Brian F. Schaffner, and Sam Luks, Cambridge, MA: Harvard University, http://cces.gov.harvard.edu

views of this crucial religious voting bloc. Comparing white evangelical Republicans who were pro-choice but anti-immigration to those who are pro-life and pro-immigration reveals that Donald Trump's approval rating among both groups was statistically the same—right around 89 percent. If the prevailing wisdom were correct and white evangelicals supported President Trump because of his stated goal of appointing pro-life justices, then we should see his approval rating depend, at least in part, on the abortion views of white evangelicals. Instead, we don't see that at all.

CONCLUSIONS

The overarching sense that the data provides in this case is that abortion does not hold some kind of special place in the mind of white evangelical voters. Instead, I think there's fairly convincing evidence that, at least in the case of Donald Trump, his support was predicated at least as much on his position on immigration as it was on the topic of abortion. In myth 2, I noted that Donald Trump was the choice of the majority of evangelicals at nearly all worship attendance levels in the Republican primary. If abortion were the key issue for white evangelicals and immigration was of less concern, then why did more of them not support someone like Ted Cruz? Cruz had all the bona fides of an evangelical politician as a member of a Southern Baptist Church who was fond of quoting Scripture from memory on the campaign trail. The difference seems to be that Cruz was less forceful on immigration.[27] He spoke in favor of expanding the use of visas for foreign workers but changed his stance weeks before the New Hampshire primary when he was criticized by influential Republican Michelle Malkin for not being conservative enough.

I think it's much more statistically accurate to say that white evangelical Republicans place a high value on a number of policies, immigration and abortion chief among them. To be a Republican candidate running for statewide office is to favor policies that would restrict if not outright ban abortion. Thus, abortion is not an issue that differentiates one candidate from another. Instead, Republican politicians are pivoting to other policy arenas that may win over other voting blocs. Donald Trump had a great deal of success by focusing on immigration when other candidates did not. That proved to be a winning strategy and also exposed the fact that abortion does not hold some special place in politics for white evangelicals.

For Further Reading

Lewis, Andrew R. *The Rights Turn in Conservative Christian Politics: How Abortion Transformed the Culture Wars*. Cambridge University Press, 2017.

Lewis argues that Christian conservatives have begun to see sustained success in the courts by shifting their focus to religious freedom, rather than the details of issues such as gay marriage or abortion. In doing so, evangelical lawyers have managed to win over public opinion and rack up victories in cases at all levels of the judicial system.

Martí, Gerard. *American Blindspot: Race, Class, Religion, and the Trump Presidency*. Lanham, MD: Rowman & Littlefield Publishers, 2019.

Gerardo Marti lays out a much more nuanced version of how race, class, and religion interacted to give the White House to Donald Trump in 2016. Marti weaves together historical accounts with recent social science data to help the reader understand the ascendancy of Donald Trump.

Yukich, Grace. *One Family under God: Immigration Politics and Progressive Religion in America*. Oxford University Press. 2013.

In this accessible book, Yukich describes the tension between faith and immigration policy. People are often angered by what they perceive as a broken immigration system but are also unwilling to articulate just how immigration policy should be changed and how rule breakers should be punished.

White evangelicals agree with the Republican party only on social issues

IN THE EARLY 1990S, THE FUTURE OF THE REPUB-
lican Party looked incredibly strong. The country had experienced
eight years of Ronald Reagan as the economy boomed in the
1980s and the Communist bloc began to falter under the weight
of its own bureaucracy. Thus, it only made sense that Reagan's
vice president, George H. W. Bush, would run to succeed him on
the Republican ticket. Bush pulled out a victory in the 1988 presidential election against Democrat Michael Dukakis, and everyone
assumed the party would support Bush's bid for reelection.

But something happened in 1992 that very few anticipated:
the sitting president faced a primary challenge from a political
novice, Pat Buchanan. Buchanan had made a name for himself
in the world of media and political consulting but had never held
elected office when he decided to campaign hard for the Republican nomination. Buchanan's angle of attack against Bush was
simply that the sitting president was not conservative enough.
Buchanan believed that legal immigration should be reduced in
the United States, that abortion should be completely outlawed in
all fifty states, and that there should be a constitutional amendment establishing that legal marriage could be between only one
man and one woman.

Buchanan's insistence that mainstream Republicans were not conservative enough had gained some traction because the Bush administration had promised that there would be no increase in taxes yet signed a bill in 1990 that raised the individual income tax rate. Thus, Buchanan led an insurgency movement that caused real concern among the Bush campaign team. The upstart candidate managed to garner at least 30 percent of the primary vote in New Hampshire and a number of other key states, such as Georgia, Florida, and Colorado. It took until March for Buchanan's support to finally fade and Bush to emerge as the consensus nominee.[28]

Wanting to throw a bone to the conservative wing of the Republican party, the Bush campaign team agreed to give Pat Buchanan a prime-time speaking slot at the Republican National Convention in August. The address Buchanan delivered would become a turning point in American political discourse. The fiery conservative said, "There is a religious war going on in this country. It is a cultural war, as critical to the kind of nation we shall be as the Cold War itself." Historians refer to this as the "Culture War" speech, and Buchanan used his time on stage to rail against what he saw was an increasingly liberal Democratic Party led by Bill and Hillary Clinton. In the most telling passage, Buchanan states:

> This, my friends, is radical feminism. The agenda that Clinton & Clinton would impose on America: abortion on demand, a litmus test for the Supreme Court, homosexual rights, discrimination against religious schools, women in combat units. That's change, all right. But that's not the kind of change America needs. It's not the kind of change America wants. And it's not the kind of change we can abide in a nation we still call "God's country."[29]

Thus, Buchanan gave voice to an idea that had been percolating among political pundits for a while: many Republicans voted for the GOP not because of their views of fiscal or trade policy, but instead for what Buchanan would describe as "culture war" issues. A new army of so-called values voters began to emerge, dead set on electing Republicans who would outlaw abortion and pornography and would never allow any government entity to recognize a same-sex union. Many political observers, such as Thomas Frank, whom I mentioned in myth 12, argue that white evangelicals are a specific type of Republican—very conservative on social issues but less in lockstep on taxation and regulation. However, digging into the data just a little bit tells a much different story. In fact, there's not that much daylight between the average white evangelical Republican and the rest of the GOP on almost every issue.

Fortunately, a plethora of survey data was gathered about how individuals felt on a wide variety of social, economic, and cultural issues in the run-up to the 2020 presidential election. I compared those who identified as white evangelical Republicans to all the other Republicans in the sample by examining some of the issues that Pat Buchanan referred to in his famous 1992 speech. This is visualized in figure 12.1. While the terms of the debate obviously evolved in more than a quarter century, voters in 2020 were still thinking about the inclusion of religion in public schools, a woman's ability to obtain an abortion, and issues surrounding sexuality.

There's clear evidence here that white evangelicals do differ from other Republicans when it comes to social issues; however, the size of those gaps does vary based on the specific issue. For instance, it makes sense that 91 percent of white evangelical Republicans want to place the Ten Commandments in school buildings, but that policy is also supported by 78 percent of Republicans who are not white evangelicals, a thirteen-point gap. When it comes to support for transgender troops in the military, 46 percent are in favor—about thirteen points lower than non-evangelicals. On the issue of legalizing marijuana, the gap between these two groups is eight percentage points—and half of white

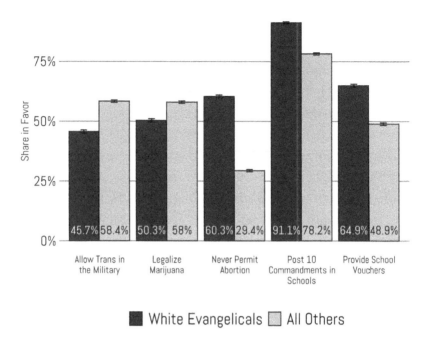

Figure 12.1. Social Issue Support among Republicans

Data from the Nationscape Survey, administered by the Democracy Fund's Voter Study Group. Los Angeles: University of California. https://www.voter-studygroup.org/data

evangelical Republicans support marijuana legalization efforts. There's also a sixteen-point gap on the topic of school vouchers.

However, clearly the largest difference between white evangelical Republicans and the rest of the Republican party in pure statistical terms is on abortion. A white evangelical Republican was twice as likely to want to ban abortion completely than a Republican who is not a white evangelical. Taken together there is some evidence here that white evangelical Republicans are categorically distinct from other Republicans when it comes to classic culture-war issues.

Thus, it's fair to say that white evangelical Republicans are noticeably more conservative on social issues such as abortion, sexuality, and religion in public schools. But is there any basis for believing that white evangelicals should be to the right of the GOP on other issues that are not so strongly linked to theological matters? Political observers such as Thomas Frank contend that white evangelicals are only thinking of social issues when they enter the voting booth and are finding ways to justify or explain away the Republican Party's position on immigration, taxation, and other areas of public policy.[30] But the data tells a far different story. White evangelical Republicans are at least as conservative as the rest of the Republican base on a whole host of issues. In fact, on immigration they are noticeably more to the right of non-evangelical Republicans.

For instance, as can be seen in figure 12.2, 85 percent of white evangelical Republicans support building a wall on the Southern

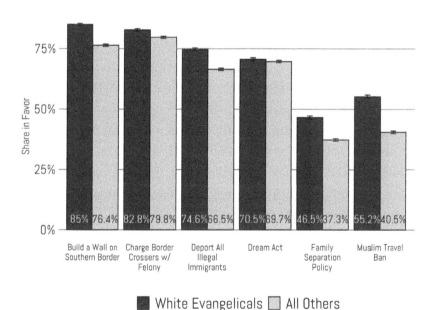

Figure 12.2. Immigration Issue Support among Republicans

Data from the Nationscape Survey, administered by the Democracy Fund's Voter Study Group. Los Angeles: University of California. https://www.voter-studygroup.org/data

border, as 76 percent of the rest of the Republican party does. Three-quarters of white evangelical Republicans want to deport all illegal immigrants, it's two-thirds of the rest of the party. On family separation, white evangelicals supported Trump's policy at a rate nine points higher than the rest of the GOP. And 55 percent of white evangelical Republicans were in favor of a Muslim travel ban, fifteen points higher than all the others in the Republican coalition.

Looked at in its totality, there's clear evidence here that white evangelical Republicans are more conservative on immigration policy than the rest of the Republican party. In some cases, those gaps are fairly large. These results—including data from myth 11 that indicates immigration is just as important as abortion and myth 2, which indicates that Donald Trump, a candidate who proposed a Muslim travel ban a month before the New Hampshire primary, was the frontrunner in the Republican primary among white evangelicals—provide a fairly compelling argument for the centrality of immigration to white evangelical Republicans.

What role does economic policy play in separating white evangelical Republicans from other Republicans? Across the nine economic policies included in the Nationscape survey—including taxation, minimum wage hikes, and providing more support to new parents that are visualized in figure 12.3—there's little evidence that white evangelicals differ in any meaningful way from Republicans with other religious backgrounds.

For instance, 49 percent of white evangelical Republicans support a policy that would allow all students to graduate from state colleges debt free. That's not statistically different from the 50 percent of the rest of the GOP who support that proposal. Sixty-nine percent of white evangelical Republicans support paid maternity leave, which is not materially different from the 72 percent of non-white evangelicals who support the same policy. In no instance is the gap between the two groups more than four percentage points.

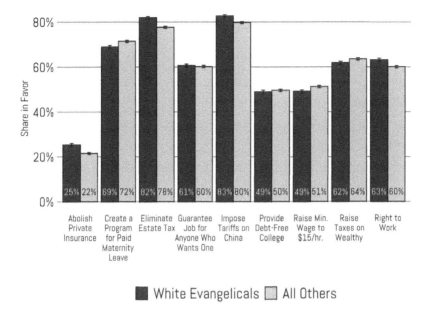

White Evangelicals ☐ **All Others**

Figure 12.3. Economic Issue Support among Republicans

Data from the Nationscape Survey, administered by the Democracy Fund's Voter Study Group. Los Angeles: University of California. https://www.voter-studygroup.org/data

There are two main conclusions that could be drawn from these results on economic policy. The first is that the economic views of white evangelical Republicans are not substantively different from the rest of the population that aligns with the GOP. However, the other conclusion is just how popular many of these proposals are with Republican voters. About seven in ten Republicans support paid maternity leave. Nearly two-thirds support raising taxes on the wealthy. The party is evenly divided on the issue of raising the minimum wage to $15 per hour. That's strong evidence that rank-and-file GOP voters want more government intervention with the economy. It's notable how large the disconnect is between Republican leadership and GOP voters on these policies.

CONCLUSIONS

Having examined how both evangelical and non-evangelical Republican voters view social issues, immigration, and economic policy, there's little reason to believe that white evangelicals are just voting for the Republican party because they want to protect the life of the unborn or are fighting to have more Judeo-Christian displays in public school. Instead, a more complete description about white evangelical Republicans is that they are at least as conservative as the average GOP identifier, but on policies relating to immigration, they are actually to the right of the median Republican.

Obviously that's to be expected when it comes to issues like abortion and transgender individuals in the military. However, the reasons for white evangelical Republicans to be even more conservative on immigration seemed to be less rooted in theological concerns and more tied into the current political climate in the United States. In some ways, this is the strongest evidence of how influential Donald Trump has been on the white evangelical base that is so central to the Republican party. In 2020, nearly half of the entire Republican coalition was made up of evangelical voters.

There's an old adage among people who study political behavior: party identification is the most powerful force in the world. That seems applicable here. Why do white evangelical Republicans hold conservative views on immigration and economics? It's because they are Republicans and the GOP's view of these issues is conservative. It's fair to assume that many white evangelicals were drawn to the GOP over culture war issues while disagreeing on economic policy during the time of Pat Buchanan, but that's just not the case any longer.

Instead of being single-issue voters, what seems to be happening is that slowly and surely, individuals begin to shift their perspectives on all issues to align with the prevailing wisdom in their party. If an individual started listening to partisan talk radio or watching a specific cable news network because they were initially intrigued by the rhetoric on abortion or gay marriage, they were still exposed to discussion of other issues like immigration and taxation. This repeated exposure over a long period of time would likely change anyone's view of these other issues. Thus, evangelicals may have started out as "values voters," but now they are the core of the Republican Party—toeing the line on economic policy and maybe even pulling the GOP to the right on immigration over the past few years.

For Further Reading

Balmer, Randall. "The Real Origins of the Religious Right," *Politico Magazine*, 2014, https://www.politico.com/magazine/story/2014/05/religious-right-real-origins-107133/. Accessed July 6, 2021.

In this long-form essay for *Politico* magazine, Randall Balmer makes a stirring argument that the idea that the religious right was founded as a backlash against Roe v. Wade is patently false. Instead, Balmer believes that the foundation of the religious right was formed through a series of battles over racial integration. According to Balmer, evangelicals were ambivalent about politics until the Supreme Court ordered schools to become racially diverse.

Kruse, Kevin M. *One Nation Under God: How Corporate America Invented Christian America*. New York: Basic Books, 2015.

The Princeton historian Kevin Kruse offers a fascinating thesis on the formation of the religious right that is not primarily based on culture war issues. In this book, Kruse contends that what really accelerated the growth of Christian conservatives was the financial backing that big business offered pastors to extol the values of the free market. For Kruse, evangelicalism and capitalism are more closely linked than most Americans have ever really considered.

Smillie, Dirk. *Falwell Inc.: Inside a Religious, Political, Educational, and Business Empire*. New York: Macmillan, 2008.

To understand how the religious right emerged, it's crucial to get a sense of how its most important figure, Jerry Falwell, rose to national prominence. This biography goes into great detail about how Falwell built a media empire in the 1960s and 1970s and parlayed that into a number of ventures, including the founding of Liberty University.

Most Catholics and evangelicals do not support women in leadership

ONE OF THE HARDEST JOBS FOR SCHOLARS OF American religion is to try to generate a classification scheme of religious groups that is not overly reductive but not so complicated that it's impossible to remember. The trade-offs between simplicity and overgeneralization are very real when it comes to sorting Protestant Christianity into a small number of groups that tend to have similar views of theology and politics. The most widely accepted way to accomplish this task is to divide the predominantly white traditions into two distinct groups: evangelicals and mainline Protestants. Most Americans seem to have a solid grasp of what an evangelical is from casually observing media reports on religion and politics, but most people have never heard the term "mainline Protestant." Whenever I post on Twitter a visualization that contains that term, someone will ask in the comments what a mainline Protestant is.

When people ask me how they would know if they are an evangelical or a mainline Protestant, I find that many of the academic explanations seem disconnected from what they see as a member of a local church. The question I have found that cuts through all the noise of mainline versus evangelical is a simple one: Can a woman preach the Sunday sermon at your church? While not a perfect approximation of the divide between mainline and evangelical, the issue of women clergy is surely the most visible manifestation of the differences between the two types of white Protestant Christianity. If your church can have a female pastor, it is more than likely mainline. If that's forbidden, then there's a very good chance it's an evangelical congregation.

To support their position, evangelicals rely on several verses in the New Testament, the clearest of which is 1 Timothy 2:12: "I do not permit a woman to teach or to assume authority over a man; she must be quiet." Mainline Protestants say such verses may have been applicable in that particular first-century community but are no longer relevant to the modern church. Evangelicals take this and other verses literally and thus disqualify women from ordained ministry. Thus, this debate over women in leadership is symbolic of the bigger divide between mainline Protestants, who believe that the Bible should be interpreted in the broader context of Scripture as a whole, as well as in its cultural context, and evangelicals, who believe that each verse should be taken as what they consider to be the literal word of God.

The largest Protestant denomination in the United States is the Southern Baptist Convention. One way that they managed to get to over sixteen million members is by carving out their own very conservative niche in the American religious landscape. One of the most visible manifestations of that is that Southern Baptists take a hard line on women pastors. The Baptist Faith and Message, a summary of Baptist thought, was revised in 2000 to make the clear claim, "While both men and women are gifted for service in the church, the office of pastor is limited to men as qualified by Scripture."[31] One of the most prominent voices in the Convention, Al Mohler, has consistently stated that he believes that evangelicalism has maintained its size while many mainline traditions have seen tremendous declines in membership because of evangelicalism's conservative positions on things like women as pastors.

That's not to say that evangelicals are the only Christian tradition that prohibits women from ordained or other leadership. The Catechism of the Catholic Church states, "The Church has no authority whatsoever to confer priestly ordination on women and that this judgment is to be definitively held by all the Church's faithful." Pope Francis, who is seen by many as a less conservative leader of the Catholic Church, was asked about the issue by a reporter in 2013. He responded, "The church has spoken and says no.... That door is closed."[32]

Thus, between evangelicalism and the Catholic Church, about 45 percent of Americans are affiliated with a faith tradition that does not grant women full access to leadership. But do the people in the pews of the average evangelical or Catholic Church actually agree that women shouldn't have access to leadership roles in the church community? If you read the writings and listen to the sermons of leaders in these traditions, they often assume there's unanimity among the laity on this issue and that the position is one of the things that make them distinct.

The assumption is that people who attend these types of churches do so because they agree with the doctrines of that faith tradition. Leaders in both traditions operate from the position that if people didn't agree with that view, then they wouldn't show up at worship each Sunday. The data tells a much different story, however. Significant numbers of Catholics and evangelicals support women in all facets of church leadership, and it's nearly impossible to find any subgroup in which support for female clergy drops below 50 percent.

In March 2020, a number of colleagues and I pooled our resources to put together a survey of the general public that included a battery of questions about women in church leadership.

We began this section of the survey with the following sentence: "Assuming the women in question have appropriate training and certification, please indicate how much you agree or disagree with the following statements." The four statements were:

1. Women should be allowed to teach children's religious education classes.
2. Women should be allowed to lead congregational singing during worship services.
3. Women should be allowed to preach during women's conferences or retreats.
4. Women should be allowed to preach behind the pulpit in worship services.

They were intentionally ordered this way, as we assumed that very few evangelicals would object to the first statement (women teaching Sunday school), but many more would object to the last one (women preaching in worship). What we found contradicted the assumptions that we all had made about the support for women in church leadership.

In the general sample there's widespread support for women in all leadership roles as can be seen in figure 13.1. Eighty-three percent believe women should be able to teach Sunday school, and three-quarters of the general public support women preaching during Sunday services. However, that general sample contains people who are religiously unaffiliated or are not part of a Christian tradition. What about Catholics? The data indicates that ordinary Catholics are strongly opposed to the position held to by the Vatican. In fact, there's some evidence that Catholics are slightly more supportive of women in leadership than the general public.

The bar graph on the right shows responses of those who self-identified as evangelical Christians. Note how there is no

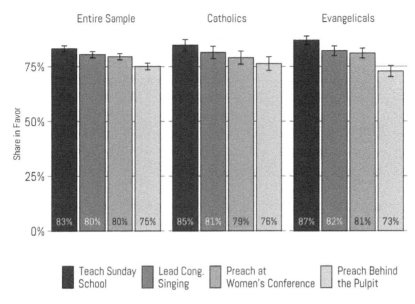

Figure 13.1. Support for Women in Church Leadership

Data from a survey fielded in Fall 2019 by Paul Djupe (Denison University) and Ryan Burge. The survey was administered by Qualtrics and contained a random sample of 3,136 respondents. The data will be available for download in the future.

substantive difference between the views of evangelicals and the general public on women taking on leadership roles. Eighty-seven percent of evangelicals think women should be able to teach at Sunday school, and 73 percent support a woman preaching the Sunday sermon. It's fair to say that in the average evangelical congregation, those who support women in leadership outnumber those who hold to the traditional evangelical position three to one.

Maybe the issue, however, is that those who are members of the Catholic Church or the evangelical tradition but do not attend services regularly are skewing the numbers. It would seem logical that those who are in the pews every weekend at Mass or Sunday service are the ones who hold more closely to the doctrines

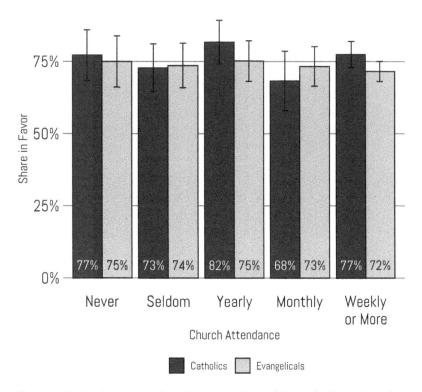

Figure 13.2. Support for Women Preaching during Worship Services

Data from a survey fielded in Fall 2019 by Paul Djupe (Denison University) and Ryan Burge. The survey was administered by Qualtrics and contained a random sample of 3,136 respondents. The data will be available for download in the future.

of their faith tradition. To test that, I broke the sample down by self-reported church attendance and looked specifically at the question of women preaching during the weekend service. The results in figure 13.2 are surprising.

Among Catholics who never attend Mass, 77 percent favored a woman preaching the homily during Mass. Among Catholics who attended Mass at least once a week, 77 percent supported a woman preaching the homily. Among never-attending evangelicals, 75 percent supported a woman preaching the Sunday sermon. Among evangelicals who attended church at least once per week, 72 percent supported a woman in the pulpit. In short, there's no discernible difference in support for women pastors based on church attendance. The simplest, most statistically accurate conclusion is that about 75 percent of Catholics and evangelicals support a woman preaching, regardless of how often they go to church and that church attendance has no bearing on the views of Catholics and evangelicals toward women in church leadership.

It's possible more opposition could be uncovered if the sample was broken down by respondents' view of the Bible. Recall that evangelicals take a more literalist approach to Scripture, which justifies their opposition to female preachers. The survey asked respondents their thoughts about the Bible. The sample was divided into those who believed the Bible should be taken literally and those who did not. I also broke the sample up by gender, theorizing that women express stronger support for female church leaders than their male counterparts.

As is shown in figure 13.3, among Catholic or evangelical men who are biblical literalists, 75 percent support women preaching during a worship service. That's actually five points higher than

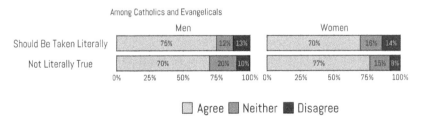

Figure 13.3. Women Should Be Allowed to Preach during Worship Services by View of the Bible

Data from a survey fielded in Fall 2019 by Paul Djupe (Denison University) and Ryan Burge. The survey was administered by Qualtrics and contained a random sample of 3,136 respondents. The data will be available for download in the future.

men who are not biblical literalists. Among women, 70 percent of Catholic or evangelical biblical literalists believe women should have access to the pulpit. That rises to 77 percent among women who don't think that the Bible should be taken literally. Trying to find a combination of demographic and religious factors to get support for women preaching to drop below 70 percent is nearly impossible. In short, support for women pastors is robust across gender, church attendance, and view of the Bible.

CONCLUSIONS

An obvious question emerges from these results: if large percentages of average evangelicals and Catholics support women having access to all types of church leadership, then why has it not happened? When the results of this survey were published online, the aforementioned Southern Baptist leader Al Mohler stated that he didn't believe these results. In his mind, it didn't make sense that so many Southern Baptists favored women pastors, but there weren't women leading any churches in the SBC. Recent developments seem to support the survey data, however.

Saddleback Church, one of the largest and most influential churches in the Southern Baptist Convention and led by celebrity pastor Rick Warren, ordained three women as part of their worship service on Mother's Day in 2021. The Sunday sermon that week was delivered by Pastor Warren's wife, Kay. On the same day, Second Baptist Church in Houston, Texas, another prominent member of the SBC, heard Anne Graham Lotz, the daughter of Billy Graham, preach the sermon. Ed Young, the pastor of Second Baptist, invited his congregation to attend by stating, "You will not want to miss Anne Graham Lotz, the 'best preacher' her dad Billy Graham ever heard!"

However, what may be the most significant development on this front is the departure of Beth Moore from the Southern Baptist Convention. Moore was easily the most popular female Southern Baptist in the United States, selling millions of copies of her Bible studies and speaking to crowds of hundreds of thousands per year. Not only did Moore announce that she was leaving the SBC, she also tweeted that she was now rejecting the Southern Baptist position that women cannot have access to leadership.

Thus, while the myth that evangelicals and Catholics do not support female pastors may have been widely held by many over the last several decades, views seem to be shifting rapidly as more cracks begin to form in this doctrine among evangelical traditions. It's impossible to know what exactly drove this shift, but perhaps the "Me Too" movement that turned a spotlight on how women have been abused, discriminated against, and kept from leadership in all facets of American society did not leave religious institutions unscathed. Many thoughtful Christians began to consider how their theological views of gender roles may have caused real harm to both women and men in the church, harm that may have not risen to the level of criminality but that was certainly real. Societal views of gender roles are evolving rapidly, putting evangelicals and Catholics further at odds with mainstream society. How these two religious traditions respond will likely have huge ramifications for the future of American Christianity.

For Further Reading

Brasher, Brenda. *Godly Women: Fundamentalism and Female Power*. New Brunswick, NJ: Rutgers University Press, 1997.

Brenda Brasher embedded herself in fundamentalist Christianity for six months in an attempt to understand how gender functions in conservative evangelical churches. What emerged is a fascinating case study of how those religious communities are divided based on gender lines, but women still manage to wield power in subtle, but important ways.

Chaves, Mark. *Ordaining Women: Culture and Conflict in Religious Organizations*. Cambridge, MA: Harvard University Press, 1999.

Mark Chaves is one of the most important and influential sociologists of religion in the United States. His book on the ordination of women is considered to be one of the most important academic books on the topic. Chaves approaches the issue not from a theological angle but by focusing on organizational theory. His insights are especially beneficial for those who have only approached this topic from the role of pastor or church leader.

Hoffmann, John P., and John P. Bartkowski. "Gender, Religious Tradition, and Biblical Literalism." *Social Forces* 86, no. 3 (2008): 1245–72.

In a fascinating study using quantitative data, Hoffman and Bartkowski come to a startling conclusion: women are more likely to be biblical literalists than men. The reason for this, according to the authors, is that women embrace a conservative theology as a way to compensate for their lack of access to church leadership.

White Christians have always been conservative Republicans

I WAS BORN AND RAISED IN A SMALL TOWN IN RURAL southern Illinois called Salem. If you ask a proud resident of Salem, Illinois, what the town is known for, they will usually mention something from a very short list of accomplishments. Most people love to mention that Miracle Whip was invented there. Others will note that the first draft of the GI Bill of Rights was written at the American Legion Post in Salem in 1943. However, what the town may be most known for is that it was the birthplace of William Jennings Bryan. If you are a history buff, you will no doubt have heard of Bryan, but most people are clueless when I mention his name. I don't blame them. I also rolled my eyes many times when he was brought up in history class.

The only thing I knew about him when I graduated from high school was that he was the only person to run for president three times and lose all three contests. A dubious distinction, to be sure. However, as I moved through my college career I became much more interested in Bryan's life. Despite his inability to win the White House, Bryan was one of the most famous men in America for several decades around 1900.

Bryan's final act might have been his most memorable. He was asked by the state of Tennessee to be the prosecutor in the famous Scopes Monkey Trial. That case revolved around a state law that forbade the teaching of evolution in public schools. John Scopes willfully defied that law as a way to test its constitutionality, and his trial quickly rose to national prominence. Bryan, a fundamentalist Christian, was trying to convict Scopes. He was opposed by Clarence Darrow, an avowed atheist and member of the ACLU. In the most climatic moment of the case, Darrow called Bryan himself to testify.

On direct examination, Darrow had one goal: make Bryan look foolish. He asked Bryan if he believed that Jonah was really swallowed by a whale or if God made the Earth stand still, as it is described in the book of Joshua. On both accounts, Bryan tried to be evasive but still confirmed his belief that the Bible was literally true. The media coverage was devastating for Bryan, painting him to be an unsophisticated, uneducated bigot. Although Bryan won the trial, Christianity lost the public relations battle.

When most historians think of William Jennings Bryan, they think of his religious beliefs and his time on the stand in Dayton, Tennessee. What they overlook is that William Jennings Bryan held incredibly liberal views on economic policy. He favored a federal income tax, he wanted the government to test food and drugs to ensure they were safe, and he believed that most utilities should be owned by local governments, not corporations. One of his most famous lines during his stump speech was, "No one can earn a million dollars honestly." In modern parlance, William Jennings Bryan was a fundamentalist Christian socialist.[33] It's fair to say that he would have no place in politics in the twenty-first century.

Bryan's positions on both theology and politics seem so out of place to readers in the twenty-first century because of the current landscape of the United States. In the minds of many, to be a Christian is to be a political conservative. If one were asked to name a Christian fundamentalist, many would probably mention Pat Robertson or Jerry Falwell. Both men were well known for their outspoken support of the Republican Party. In fact, it's nearly impossible to name a conservative evangelical who has not publicly pledged their support for the GOP. Thus, many people equate conservative religious beliefs (specifically white Christianity) with conservative political views. But that has not always been the case. In fact, Democrats outnumbered Republicans among white Christians as late as the 1980s.

The first year of the General Social Survey was 1972, and among white respondents who attended religious services nearly once a week or more, 56 percent were Democrats and 34 percent were Republicans, with 10 percent identifying as political Independents, as can be seen in figure 14.1. By 1986 a significant shift already occurred, with Republicans making up a larger share of devout

Partisanship of White Weekly Church Goers

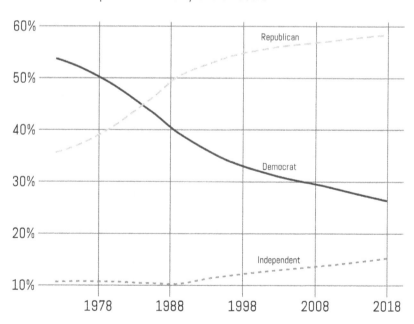

Figure 14.1. Partisanship of White Weekly Churchgoers

Data from the General Social Survey, a project of the independent research organization NORC at the University of Chicago, with principal funding from the National Science Foundation, https://gss.norc.org/Get-The-Data

white Christians than Democrats (45 percent vs. 42 percent). That trend only accelerated from there. Just ten years later, Republicans were 53 percent of white weekly churchgoers compared to only 37 percent who were Democrats. By 2018, the gap between Republicans and Democrats had grown to more than forty percentage points (63 percent Republicans compared to only 22 percent Democrats).

Some astute observers of American religion and politics would look at this analysis and believe that the sharp rightward movement of white weekly church attenders is due to evangelicals becoming even more closely linked with the GOP. However, when this group of white Christians is broken up into evangelicals, mainline Protestants, and Catholics, it becomes clear that the story is a bit more complicated, as seen in figure 14.2.

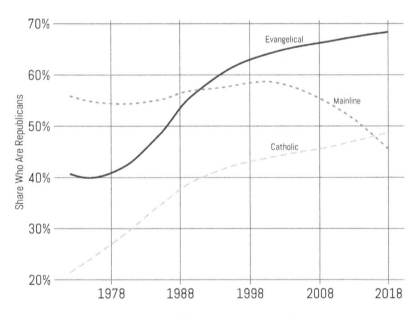

Figure 14.2. Republican Affiliation of White Weekly Churchgoers by Tradition

Data from the General Social Survey, a project of the independent research organization NORC at the University of Chicago, with principal funding from the National Science Foundation, https://gss.norc.org/Get-The-Data

It's clear that white evangelicals have moved significantly toward the Republican party in the past forty-six years. In the 1970s, about 40 percent of white evangelicals who went to church weekly identified as Republicans. In 2018, that had risen to nearly 70 percent. However, they are not alone in this shift toward the right. White Catholics have also shifted their political allegiance over the past four decades. In the early 1970s, less than a quarter of devout white Catholics were Republicans. But by 1990, that share had jumped to about 40 percent. That rate of movement toward the GOP did slow significantly over the next twenty-eight years, but by 2018 nearly half of white Catholics were Republicans.

The only group that goes the other direction is mainline Protestants. For decades a bare majority of United Methodists, Episcopalians, and other moderate Protestants were aligned with the GOP. That actually rose to nearly 60 percent right around 2000. But from that point forward, devout mainliners have moved away from the Republican party. By 2018, just over 45 percent of mainliners were Republicans, the lowest percentage in the forty-six-year history of the GSS. But as will be discussed in myth 18, mainliners represent only a small portion of the American population compared to evangelicals and Catholics. Thus, their fifteen-point swing to the left is dwarfed by the rightward movement of the other Christian traditions.

But note that up to this point, the analysis has focused on only one way to measure this phenomenon: political partisanship. Political science also recognizes that political ideology is another way in which people perceive the political landscape. This question asks respondents how they identify on a range from "extremely liberal" to "extremely conservative" with "moderate" being the middle option. While significant shares of white weekly churchgoers did align with the Democratic party in the 1970s and 1980s, white Christians have always hesitated to embrace the term "liberal."

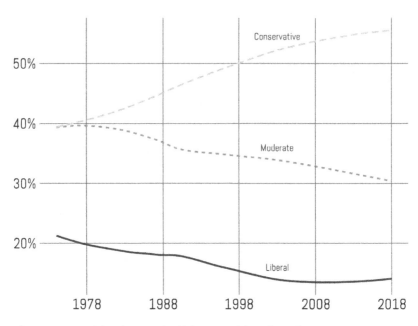

Figure 14.3. Ideology of White Weekly Churchgoers

Data from the General Social Survey, a project of the independent research organization NORC at the University of Chicago, with principal funding from the National Science Foundation, https://gss.norc.org/Get-The-Data

Recall that over half of white weekly church attenders aligned with the Democratic party in 1972. But it's notable that just 21 percent of this group described their ideology as liberal at the same time in figure 14.3. And, in fact, that was the high watermark for the term "liberal." In 2018, just 14 percent of white weekly churchgoers referred to themselves as liberals. It's also worth considering that in the 1970s, white weekly attending Christians were just as likely to describe their ideology as moderate as they were to describe it as conservative. That quickly changed through the 1980s, though.

By 1988, 37 percent of white weekly churchgoing Christians said they were moderates, and 45 percent claimed they were conservatives, a gap of eight percentage points. Ten years later the size of that gulf had doubled to 15 percent. By 2008, 53 percent said they were conservatives and 33 percent, moderates. In the most recent data collected from 2018, 55 percent of white weekly church attendees said they were conservative, and only 30 percent indicated they were moderate.

Visualizing how both ideology and political partisanship come together through the three white Protestant traditions is helpful in understanding how much movement has occurred and in which direction. To do so, I measure the mean partisanship and ideology at five points in time: 1978, 1988, 1998, 2008, and 2018 (figure 14.4).

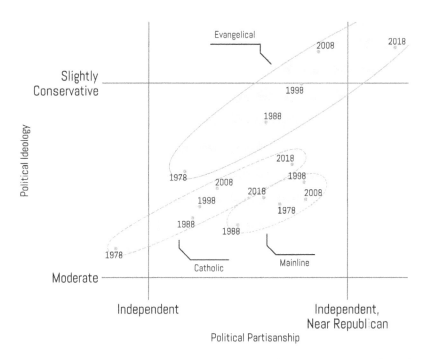

Figure 14.4. Movement of White Weekly Churchgoers in Political Space (1978–2018)

Data from the General Social Survey, a project of the independent research organization NORC at the University of Chicago, with principal funding from the National Science Foundation, https://gss.norc.org/Get-The-Data

When seen from this view, it becomes clear that both white Catholics and white evangelicals moved nearly the same distance between 1978 and 2018; however, the starting points for the traditions are different. Catholics in 1978 were more moderate and further to the left on the partisan spectrum than white evangelicals during the same time period. But by 2018, the average white Catholic who goes to Mass weekly was more Republican than a weekly attending white evangelical in 1988. However, it's crucial to note that the movement for white Catholics is more about a shift in partisanship than it is a change in ideology.

It's clear white evangelicals as a group are an outlier even compared to mainline Protestants and Catholics, though. No group has ever been as conservative or Republican as white evangelicals were from 2008 onward. It's also worth pointing out that the distance white evangelicals moved on the partisan dimension between 2008 and 2018 is nearly as large as the movement they made between 1978 and 1988. Mainline Protestants, on the other hand, have moved very little on either axis. In fact, their movements do not shift in one clear direction. Instead, they jump leftward from 1978 to 1988 but then go back to the right in the next decade.

CONCLUSION

Hundreds of articles have been written to explain how white Christians, who used to be fairly evenly divided between the parties, have now become solidly Republican, especially in rural areas and the southern United States. There's obviously no single reason for this dramatic shift over the past five decades, but a good place to start would be with what historians have dubbed "The Southern Strategy."

Many white southerners were solid Democrat voters beginning in the 1930s and extending into the 1960s. This was due,
in no small part, to the popularity of Franklin Roosevelt's New
Deal, which brought a great deal of economic relief to working
class southerners. They rewarded the Democrats with their votes
for decades until things began to shift in the 1950s. When the
Supreme Court unanimously ruled in *Brown v. Board of Education*
that public schools should be racially integrated, it was an inflec-
tion point for southern society, as many southerners were sending
their children to schools that were completely racially segregated.

With the passage of the Civil Rights and the Voting Rights Acts
in the mid-1960s by President Lyndon Johnson, the resentment
many southerners felt for the Democratic party only intensified.
Republican strategists capitalized on this growing anger by positioning the party in opposition to the Democrats' view on race.
When Richard Nixon ran for president in 1968, he spoke in favor
of "state's rights" and "law and order." Both were thinly veiled
support for southern states' desire to maintain Jim Crow laws
and crush racial protests by any means necessary. By the late
1970s, the South had completely switched its political allegiance
from being strongly Democratic to the new base of support for
the Republican party. Southern white Christians were no longer
FDR Democrats but instead had formed an alliance with the
GOP—one that has only strengthened in the past four decades.

That's not to say that all the shifts seen in the data can be
explained by white Christians changing their minds about politics.
In fact, political science has shown, fairly convincingly, that very
few people truly change their political partisanship as adults.
What is more likely happening is generational replacement. The
data collected in the 1970s was filled with people who had lived
through the Great Depression and had experienced the impact of
the New Deal programs. By the 1990s, many of those voters had
died off and were being replaced by younger white Christians,

who had no memory of those events from the 1930s. Instead, they were only aware of the fights over desegregation, racial protests, and a Republican party that said it wanted states to make decisions about things like busing and voting laws.

Thus, American politics in the new millennium is more polarized on political and religious lines than ever before. In the minds of most white Americans, to be a Christian is to vote for the Republican party, while the Democrats have become the party of secular voters. Conservative atheists and socialist evangelicals find no place feels like home for them. If William Jennings Bryan were alive today, it's fair to assume that he would feel politically adrift as well.

For Further Reading

Claassen, Ryan. *Godless Democrats and Pious Republicans?: Party Activists, Party Capture, and the 'God Gap'*. Cambridge University Press, 2015.

There's a conventional wisdom that evangelicals became politically activated through the mobilization efforts of Christian organizations like the Moral Majority. Claassen rejects that narrative, believing that the primary reason that the alliance between evangelicals and the GOP has grown so strong is because evangelicals have gotten more educated and earned more money.

Green, John Clifford, James L. Guth, Corwin E. Smidt, and Lyman A. Kellstedt. *Religion and the Culture Wars: Dispatches from the Front*. Lanham, MD: Rowman & Littlefield, 1996.

Although this book is over twenty-five years old now, it's still seen as a classic text in American religion and politics. The authors of this text are pioneers in the field, and this serves as their most enduring work. Organized as a series of essays, they offer a fascinating peek into how political science understood the religious world in the 1990s and many of the theories that they offered up in this work are still being tested and debated in contemporary political science.

Layman, Geoffrey. *The Great Divide: Religious and Cultural Conflict in American Party Politics*. Columbia University Press, 2001.

While written more than two decades ago, it appears that Geoffrey Layman had a bit of crystal ball when looking at the future of religion and politics. Layman's text begins to trace some of the earliest fractures of the American electorate in those who are incredibly devout on one side and those who are entirely secular on the other.

The growth of the nones is largely from people leaving church

OVER THE PAST FEW YEARS, I'VE BEEN A GUEST ON several radio shows across the country. When I call into the station the producer typically tells me two things: how long my segment is going to be and how many seconds until I go live. I know I will have to think and talk quickly to get my point across in eight or ten minutes of airtime. Usually I have about fifteen seconds to gather myself before I go live, which feels like I get shot out of a cannon. In that fifteen-second window, there's often some type of music playing that transitions the listener from the commercial break back to live radio. At least half the time I hear the song "Losing My Religion," the 1991 hit by the band R.E.M.

I understand the choice, and I think the song is a truly great one, but it reinforces a myth that seems to be incredibly pervasive in American culture—huge shares of people are leaving the religion they were raised in to join the ranks of the religiously unaffiliated. One of the primary reasons this perception is so widespread is that we have all heard stories of friends or family who grew up in a devoutly religious home only to leave that faith tradition entirely as they moved into adulthood. Often, these stories are both heartbreaking and compelling. Tales of abuse, control, and neglect are often punctuated by a moment when a young person realizes that religion doesn't work for them anymore and they walk away.

However, the survivor bias that was described in myth 10 also applies in this context. We have to be very mindful of not only the stories we hear, but also of the stories that are never told. While someone telling their history of being raised in a religiously fundamentalist household only to be ostracized as they left the church as a teenager is obviously compelling, the experience is also fairly uncommon according to the data. If people are asked on a survey to describe the religion of their youth, then also list their current faith tradition, the vast majority still align with the religion that they were raised in. And, if they do leave that tradition from their childhood, they usually do not stray far.

This pattern presents a puzzle, though. If people aren't leaving their current religion in droves, then how do social scientists explain the fact that in the early 1970s only 5 percent of people were classified as religious nones, but today at least 30 percent are?[34] Instead of deconversion being the primary contributor to the nones, the data indicates that the biggest engine of their growth is generational replacement. Every day in America, older and more religious Americans are dying off, only to be replaced by young people moving into adulthood who are less religious.

First, let's assess just how much religious switching is going on in the American population. Since its inception, the General Social Survey has been asking respondents, "In what religion were you raised?" We should rightfully assume that some Americans probably don't have perfect recall on such a question, but generally it seems reasonable to assume they could place themselves in a larger denominational family. The GSS also asks them about their current religious tradition. Looked at

	Evangelical	Mainline	Black Prot.	Catholic	Other Faith	No Religion
No Religion	19%	9%	1%	6%	7%	58%
Other Faith	4%	3%	0%	3%	78%	13%
Catholic	6%	4%	1%	76%	3%	11%
Black Prot.	7%	2%	81%	1%	3%	6%
Mainline	13%	69%	1%	5%	3%	10%
Evangelical	76%	10%	1%	3%	3%	7%

Religious Tradition Raised In

Religious Tradition as Adult

Figure 15.1. Religious Shifts from Adolescence to Adulthood

Data from the General Social Survey, a project of the independent research organization NORC at the University of Chicago, with principal funding from the National Science Foundation, https://gss.norc.org/Get-The-Data

over the forty-six-year life of the data, the amount of religious switching that has occurred is relatively small, as can be seen in figure 15.1.

For instance, about three in four people raised in an evangelical tradition are still evangelicals as adults. But if the scope is widened to how many people raised evangelical were still Christians as adults, it's right around 90 percent. Just 7.4 percent of those raised evangelical became religiously unaffiliated, and another 2.5 percent became a member of another faith tradition as an adult (Jewish, Muslim, Hindu, etc.). That same pattern holds true for people raised in other Christian traditions as well.

Despite the fact that many people assume mainline Protestant Christianity is declining and the nones are rising, it's hard to find clear evidence of mainliners leaving faith altogether in the data. About 87 percent of people raised mainline are still Christians in adulthood. For those raised in the Black Protestant tradition, just 6 percent end up as nones. For Catholics, slightly more than 11 percent do. But there's clearly no evidence here of a strong pathway between any Christian tradition and the ranks of the unaffiliated.

What's interesting to note, however, is that for people who were raised without a religious affiliation, just 58 percent of them still claimed that they were a none as an adult. That's easily the lowest retention rate of any tradition. Of those raised nones, about 20 percent became evangelical as an adult, with another 9 percent becoming mainline and 6 percent becoming Catholic. Summed up, over 35 percent of people raised nones became Christians as adults.

It is important to mention that retention rates have shifted fairly significantly over the past four decades. I calculated the share of respondents who stayed in the same tradition in which they were raised in each decade beginning in the 1970s, and there are clear trends for many Christian groups, as is visualized in figure 15.2.

For instance, among those responding to the GSS in the 1970s, overall retention was higher than it was in more recent waves of the survey, as seen in figure 15.2. Among evangelicals, the retention rate was 76 percent in surveys from the 1970s. That has dropped to about 70 percent in more recent years. That drop looks fairly modest when comparing retention rates for other Christian traditions. For mainline Protestants, the retention rate in the 1970s was very similar to evangelicals at around 75 percent. However, mainliners have seen quite a bit more defection, with their retention rate at 56 percent in the 2010s. That same level

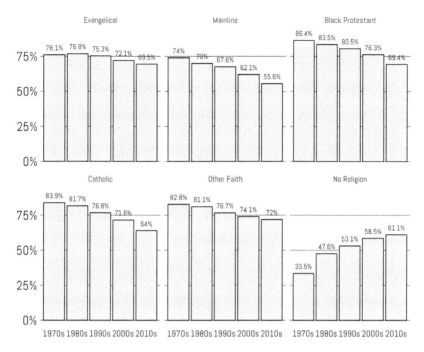

Figure 15.2. Religious Retention Rates by Decade

Data from the General Social Survey, a project of the independent research organization NORC at the University of Chicago, with principal funding from the National Science Foundation, https://gss.norc.org/Get-The-Data

of decline is apparent for Catholics as well. Eighty-four percent of people who were raised Catholic stayed in the tradition in the 1970s. More recent data indicates that the retention rate has dropped to just 64 percent.

While these retention rates have been clearly on the decline for Christian traditions, the trend is going in the opposite direction for the religiously unaffiliated. In the 1970s, just one in three people raised without a religion was still classified as a none when they were an adult. But that retention rate has steadily increased over time. By the 1990s, retention had moved above 50 percent, and in the most recent surveys, the retention rate for the nones is now north of 60 percent. That means that about three in five people who were raised without a religious affiliation stay that way through their lives now.

But even considering the fact that retention rates for many faith traditions have dipped in recent decades, there's still little evidence to indicate that the ranks of the nones are swelling by people unconverting from other faith traditions. For instance, only 13 percent of people raised evangelicals became nones in data collected since 2010. About one in five individuals raised in the mainline or Catholic tradition did. As mentioned previously, the most common story is that the people who are raised Christian will die still identifying as a Christian.

Having established that religious retention is still reasonably robust, we are still left with the bigger puzzle: why have the share of Americans with no religious affiliation risen sixfold in the last fifty years? It seems like the answer is a lot less about people unconverting and a lot more about people never being attached to religion in the first place. The data is clear on this: much larger shares of younger generations enter adulthood with no religious affiliation than ever before. They didn't leave religion; they had no faith tradition to jettison.

To assess the share of people who enter adulthood without a religious tradition, I broke the sample into five-year birth cohorts dating back to those born between 1950 and 1954. Then I calculated the share of each birth cohort who identified as religiously unaffiliated when that cohort was between the ages of 18 and 25, that is visualized in figure 15.3. My assumption is that if someone were raised with a religious tradition, they would still report an attachment to that tradition when they were young adults. If they were going to unconvert, it would happen at a point later in life. What the data reveals is that the share of people moving into adulthood without a religious attachment has tripled in the past thirty years.

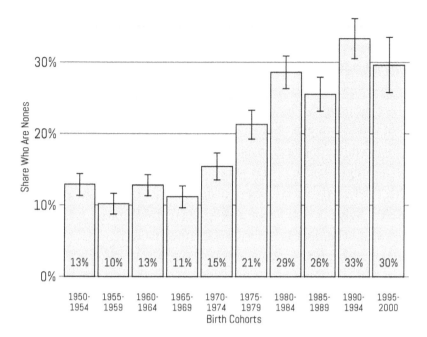

Figure 15.3. Share Who Were Nones When They Were 18–25 Years Old

Data from the General Social Survey, a project of the independent research organization NORC at the University of Chicago, with principal funding from the National Science Foundation, https://gss.norc.org/Get-The-Data

As can be observed in figure 15.3, just one in ten people born between 1955 and 1959 indicated that they had no religious affiliation when they were between the ages of eighteen and twenty-five. For the 1975 to 1979 birth cohort, the share who were nones in young adulthood had doubled to 21 percent. However, that share has risen another ten points for individuals born between 1990 and 2000. Among the Americans coming of age now, it's very likely that one in three of them were raised with no religious affiliation.

Consider what happens every single day in the United States right now—hundreds of people born in the 1930s and 1940s are dying. While we don't have data on the share of them who were nones as young adults, it stands to reason that it was likely less than 10 percent. At the same time that these older Americans are no longer counted in the United States' population, hundreds of young people who are much less religious are moving into adulthood. It doesn't take a calculator to understand that this is going to inevitably lead to Americans becoming less religious in the aggregate. When this generational replacement is coupled with the fact that somewhere around 15 to 20 percent of people raised Christian will become religiously unaffiliated as they age, the rise of the nones comes into sharper focus.

CONCLUSIONS

One very interesting implication of this analysis needs to be carefully considered, however. When just about one in twenty Americans had no religious affiliation, there was no concept of institutionalized secularism in the United States. Almost every older American who took the GSS in the 1970s said they were raised in a religious tradition. It's staggering to look at the numbers during that decade. Among people who were over the age of 55 when taking the survey, 94 percent of people indicated they were raised as a Christian, 4 percent were raised in another faith tradition. Just 2 percent said they were raised with no religious affiliation.

However, in recent years, the share who indicated the household in which they were raised was secular has risen to nearly 20 percent. In effect, what American society is seeing for the first time is second- or possibly even third-generation "none" families. Many Americans were raised as Protestants or Catholics, and many of them retain that tradition as adults more as a cultural attachment than any indication of religious devotion. However, as more and more Americans are raised without religion as young people, they will be less likely to pick a Christian tradition as the default choice when asked by a pollster what their religious affiliation is. Couple this trend with the fact that it's become much more culturally acceptable for Americans to say that they have no religious attachment, and we see a confluence of factors that leads to a skyrocketing of the nones.

This confluence of social factors opens up all kinds of interesting pathways for researchers to consider when studying American religion. Are people who were never raised with a religious tradition more open and receptive to messages from other faith groups as they move into adulthood than those who were raised in a Christian home but left that behind as they moved into their twenties and thirties? Up to this point we just didn't have enough data to answer a question like that. And for religious leaders, the challenges that face them are entirely different from just a few decades ago. Most of the literature about church growth was based on samples collected from the 1980s and 1990s. It's clear that young people in the twenty-first century have a completely different conception of religion. What new strategies will religious groups develop to attract this group? Will those new recruitment techniques slow the growth of the nones? The answers to these questions will be incredibly consequential for the trajectory of American religion.

For Further Reading

Burge, Ryan P. *The Nones: Where They Came From, Who They Are, and Where They Are Going*. Minneapolis, MN: Fortress Press, 2021.

My first book was devoted to the phenomenon of religious disaffiliation in the United States. The second chapter of the book focuses on some of the causes of the rise of the Nones and tackles arguments such as social desirability bias, secularization, and changes in family structure.

Campbell, David E., Geoffrey C. Layman, and John C. Green. *Secular Surge: A New Fault Line in American Politics*. Cambridge University Press, 2020.

Using a wealth of data from surveys the authors commissioned, a rather clear conclusion emerges: politics is driving a lot of young people away from religion. One of the clearest findings is that this religious polarization will lead to some very difficult but necessary conversations for both political parties in the near future.

Zuckerman, Phil. *Faith No More: Why People Reject Religion*. Oxford University Press, 2015.

Zuckerman is one of the most important scholars of American secularism, and this book is his most accessible look at the rise of the religiously unaffiliated in the United States. Relying on dozens of interviews with people who have left religion behind, Zuckerman finds a myriad of reasons why people leave religion, a process that often takes years. Pairing Zuckerman's insights with the quantitative data provides a balanced and illuminating view of secular Americans.

America is much less religious today than a few decades ago

I FEEL SHEEPISH WHEN I ADMIT THAT I MAY HAVE inadvertently given some ammunition to the myth that the United States is a lot less religious today than it was twenty or thirty years ago. My book *The Nones: Where They Came From, Who They Are, and Where They Are Going* was focused on the rapid increase in the share of Americans who say that they have no religious affiliation. The impetus for writing that book was a tweet I sent out in March 2019. Some new data had been released by the General Social Survey. I had analyzed it and noted that the share of Americans who indicated they had no religious affiliation was now the same size as evangelical Protestants and Catholics. That finding went viral, showing up in every major media outlet in the United States and making the front page of Reddit.

What everyone wanted to talk about was the fact that in 1972, just 5 percent of Americans said they had no religious affiliation. Today, depending on which survey instrument you use, that number is between 25 and 30 percent. Additionally, data about Generation Z indicates that over 40 percent of them claim to be atheists, agnostics, or nothing in particular. I can't blame people for just skimming the headline about the rise of the nones and concluding that religion is in terminal decline in the United States.

It is empirically correct to state that larger portions of the American population are embracing a secular identity and world-view than fifty years ago. The data is hard to dispute on this fact. But data on the rise of the nones tells only one part of the story of American religion. It would be easy to assume—after seeing charts and graphs that illustrate a decline in church attendance, a rapid rise in people expressing an atheist worldview, and fewer people identifying as Catholics and Protestants—that Americans as a whole are sliding toward secularism.

But as is the case with all things in the social world, the situation is much more nuanced than that. A more complete picture of religiosity of the United States indicates that the country is not simply headed in one direction in terms of religion. It's actually moving in two opposite directions at the same time. On one side of the religious spectrum, increasing numbers of Americans are indicating they have no belief in God, they never attend religious services, and they see themselves as atheists or agnostics. But among those who still affiliate with a religious tradition, there's fairly compelling evidence that their religiosity is at least as high as it was forty years ago. And, in some cases, they are more devout than Christians from the 1970s.

One of the most important developments in American political science literature over the past few decades is mounting evidence of political polarization. The empirical reality is that the Democratic party has moved further toward the left side of the political spectrum, while the Republicans have shifted significantly toward the right. In the 1960s and 1970s, it was not at all uncommon for members of Congress to vote for bills supported by members of the other party. Today, bipartisanship is verboten. There is no place for moderates in American politics.

But the same phenomenon seems to be occurring in American religion as well. On one side, a growing number of Americans identify as secular and eschew many of the trappings of American religion. But on the other side, a significant portion of the American population is devoutly religious. They attend church at high rates, and they have a strong belief in God. In essence, American religion has boiled down to either being very religious or being completely secular, with little in between. Thus, if the nones are parsed out of the data, a much different portrait of American religion emerges. We see the relative persistence of religion, even as American society has rapidly become more secular.

In the early 1970s, about a third of all Americans indicated they attended religious services once a week or more, as can be seen in figure 16.1. If the nones were excluded, then that share was smaller—but only by a small amount (around 31.5 percent). That reflects the fact that only 5 percent of the population indicated that they had no religious affiliation in 1972. Thus, removing this

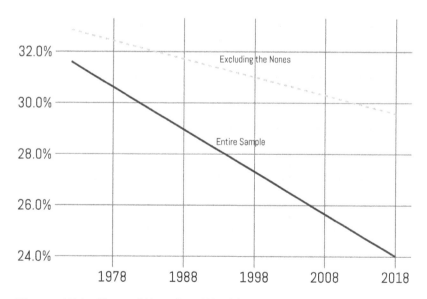

Figure 16.1. Share Attending Weekly or More

Data from the General Social Survey, a project of the independent research organization NORC at the University of Chicago, with principal funding from the National Science Foundation, https://gss.norc.org/Get-The-Data

group only has a modest impact on church attendance numbers. However, as the 1970s gave way to the 1980s, the share of the sample who claimed no religious affiliation grew, and the implications of removing them from the sample became more apparent.

By 1998, if the nones were excluded from the sample, about 31 percent of Americans indicated weekly church attendance. If the nones were still part of the sample, just about 27 percent attended weekly. That gap continued to widen over the next two decades. In the most recent data available from 2018, about 29.5 percent of Americans are weekly attenders if the nones are not included, but only 24 percent are if the entire sample is analyzed.

But it's instructive to compare the overall decline for both groups. Among the entire sample, weekly attendance dropped about 7.5 percentage points in a period of forty-six years. If the nones are omitted, the decline is much less significant (around three percentage points). For those who still maintain a religious attachment, the decline in religious practice is objectively modest. Three percentage points in forty-six years is not a sign of some type of dramatic collapse.

An even more interesting narrative emerges when analyzing the church attendance rates of the various traditions in American Christianity, as was done for figure 16.2. There's strong evidence that Protestant Christians are just as devout today as they were four decades ago, and in some cases church attendance in 2018 may be higher than it was in the early 1970s.

Among those identifying as evangelical in the 1970s, about 36 percent reported weekly church attendance. By 2018, the share of evangelicals who attended church weekly or more had risen to just over 46 percent—an increase of ten percentage points. That same upward trend appears for both Black Protestants and mainline Protestants as well, but the rise is a bit more muted. About 29 percent of Black Protestants were weekly attenders

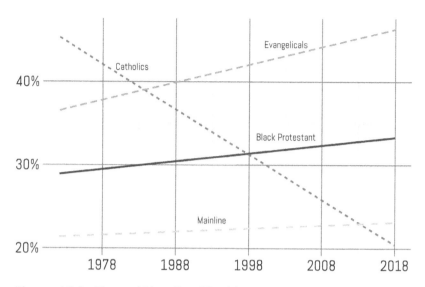

Figure 16.2. Share Attending Weekly or More

Data from the General Social Survey, a project of the independent research organization NORC at the University of Chicago, with principal funding from the National Science Foundation, https://gss.norc.org/Get-The-Data

in the 1970s. In 2018, that group was up to 33 percent. Among mainline Protestants during the same time period the share of weekly attenders rose from 21 to 23 percent.

There is a marked decline in attendance among Roman Catholic respondents, however. In 1972, about 45 percent of Catholics said they attended Mass weekly or more. By 2018, that share was only 20 percent. That trend line is in stark contrast to those from the three Protestant groups and is hard to comprehend. It may be partially related to the fact that a growing number of people embrace a type of "cultural Catholicism." According to data from the Pew Research Center, 62 percent of cultural Catholics see their attachment as more about family heritage than religious devotion. The closest parallel may be the significant number of people who identify as Jewish because of the ethnic lineage of their family but never attend synagogue.

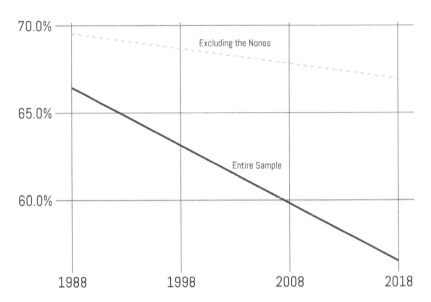

Figure 16.3. Share Believing in God without Any Doubts

Data from the General Social Survey, a project of the independent research organization NORC at the University of Chicago, with principal funding from the National Science Foundation, https://gss.norc.org/Get-The-Data

Yet religiosity is about more than just church attendance. Alongside religious behavior, there is also religious belief. The General Social Survey has been asking respondents to indicate their belief in God since 1988. The share of the sample who responded "I know God really exists and I have no doubts about it" was calculated for both the entire sample, as well as for those who still reported an affiliation with a religious tradition, and is visualized in figure 16.3.

In 1988, about two-thirds of Americans said they had no doubt God existed. But if the nones are excluded, the share is a bit higher at around 69 percent. The share of Americans who expressed a sure belief in God declined over the next three decades to about 56 percent in 2018. However, if the nones are removed from the analysis, the share of Americans who express a certain belief in

God drops only about two percentage points in thirty years. For those who still claim a religious affiliation in 2018, their beliefs look almost identical to the same group thirty years earlier.

If the sample is separated into the various traditions in Christianity, there's little evidence of a significant decline, which is apparent in figure 16.4. In 1988, just over 80 percent of evangelicals and Black Protestants indicated that they believed in God without any doubts. Thirty years later, that share was 83 percent for Black Protestants and 82 percent for evangelicals. Among mainline Protestants, there may be a one-percentage-point decline (from 59 to 58 percent in three decades). And while the share of Catholics who attend Mass weekly has dropped dramatically in the past several decades, that same pattern is much more modest when it comes to religious belief. In 1988, about two-thirds of Catholics claimed a belief in God without

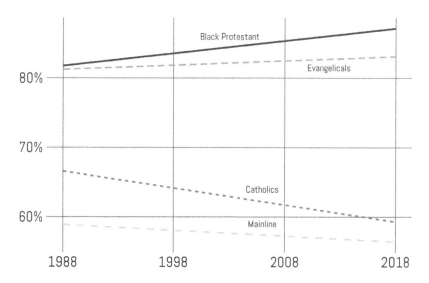

Figure 16.4. Share Believing in God without Doubt

Data from the General Social Survey, a project of the independent research organization NORC at the University of Chicago, with principal funding from the National Science Foundation, https://gss.norc.org/Get-The-Data

doubt. That dropped to about 60 percent thirty years later. Looking holistically, there's little reason to believe that Christians believe in God with any less certainty in 2018 than they did three decades earlier.

CONCLUSIONS

When I think about American religion, I am drawn to the analogy of a chef making a reduction on the stove. They typically put some type of liquid with lots of seasonings in a saucepan. They let those seasonings steep in the liquid over heat for a long period of time. As that reduction simmers over several hours, some of the liquid evaporates. In many cases, a reduction recipe calls for the sauce to reduce by half before it's ready. The chef is left with less liquid, but what remains has a much more concentrated flavor than when all the ingredients were combined at the beginning of the cooking process.

The same thing seems to be happening to American religion. Over the last several decades the heat has continually been turned up as politics has become more polarized, as people take on more commitments that make them less available to attend church services, and as rapid advances in technology make it easier than ever to entertain ourselves without leaving the comfort of home. All those factors have led significant numbers of Americans to no longer indicate a religious affiliation.

But for those who have not chosen to become a none, what is left is an even more concentrated version of American religion. People who are truly committed to their faith and who honestly believe in the doctrines and dogmas of their church are not going to leave those behind very easily. In essence, what American society has seen is that while smaller shares of Americans claim a religious affiliation, those who still choose to attach themselves to religion are the true believers. Put succinctly, American religion has become smaller but much more potent.

This situation may be creating a self-reinforcing loop among young people coming of age in 2020. While there used to be a wide variety of religious options for people, the number of viable church traditions has declined significantly. While conservative evangelicalism is still robust in the United States, this reduction process has driven out a lot of moderate Christians. Mainline Christianity (which is typified by moderate churches such as the United Methodist and the United Church of Christ) used to make up 30 percent of Americans. Today, it's just 10 percent.

Thus, many people who would like to find a church home are left with a landscape that is either theologically conservative and incredibly devout on one side or completely irreligious on the other. Left with those choices, many Americans seem to be choosing to become a none rather than an evangelical or conservative Catholic. Thus, as the middle disappears it becomes even more difficult to reverse this trend. So while those who still maintain a religious identity are more devout than ever, there are many who feel left out and spiritually homeless in the twenty-first century.

For Further Reading

Masci, David. *Who Are Cultural Catholics?* Pew Research Center, 2015, https://www.pewresearch.org/fact-tank/2015/09/03/who-are-cultural-catholics/. Accessed July 6, 2021.

Pew Research Center increasingly polls in areas that are not typically covered by academic surveys. This survey examines how cultural religion intersects with the theological positions of the Catholic Church. One notable finding: only 57 percent of cultural Catholics believe that a belief in the physical resurrection of Jesus is essential to being Catholic.

Stark, Rodney. "Secularization, RIP." *Sociology of Religion* 60, no. 3 (1999): 249–73.

Stark is without a doubt the most polarizing sociologist studying religion in the United States today. In 1999, Stark took to task the theory that societies were secularizing at a rapid rate all around the globe. While most social scientists working in this area disagree with Stark's conclusions, it's always helpful to see the other side of the argument laid out in careful detail.

Wuthnow, Robert. *Inventing American Religion: Polls, Surveys, and the Tenuous Quest for a Nation's Faith*. Oxford: Oxford University Press, 2015.

Wuthnow's work on American religion in the 1980s and 1990s is considered foundational reading in graduate seminars at universities around the world. However, in his later years, Wuthnow has begun to question some of the central assumptions of quantitative social science. His 2015 book collects his most significant doubts about the use of survey data to assess changes in American religion.

Black Protestants are political liberals

THE HARDEST PART OF MY DOCTORAL PROGRAM was taking the qualifying exams. These are done when a student has finished their coursework but hasn't yet moved on to the dissertation phase. Every school does them a bit differently, but in my doctoral program we had to sit in a row for eight hours a day, two days in a row, and answer a series of questions in our fields of expertise. They would hand you a piece of paper with three questions listed. You got to pick two and then spend the next eight hours answering them as thoroughly as you could by synthesizing all you had read in your coursework, as well as properly citing your sources. It was a brutal experience. I had compiled hundreds of index cards. On one side was the citation, and on the other there was a two-sentence summary of the work that I was supposed to memorize.

I remember waking up in the middle of the night multiple times thinking that I didn't know about some obscure area of research in political science. I would grab my note cards and continue to drill myself over and over again for months. The only way that I managed to absorb all that information was mindless repetition. I would say the citation name out loud and then talk myself through a summary of the work. I must have done that thousands of times. But apparently it worked, because I passed all three qualifying exams.

Even today, over a decade later, I can still hear those citations in my head. When a student asks me a question in class, sometimes those author names and dates will come floating back to the top of my mind, and I will drop those citations in the discussion. I've had more than one student ask, "How do you know that?" Well, somehow that qualifying exam process lodged those facts deep inside my head.

More than a dozen of those notecards contained references to work about political rhetoric and campaign messaging. Many scholars have focused on how politicians embed messages in the minds of potential voters. Some of the literature indicates that the best way to do this is through simple repetition. If a politician can link two concepts together in the minds of the average voter, they've won. Donald Trump was brilliant at doing this. When he was giving his campaign speeches, it was almost impossible for him to say the word "Democrats" without preceding it with the term "radical," "socialist," or "liberal." If you read his speeches, he uses those words dozens of times. He wanted the voters to think that Democrats had a radical ideology that was far more liberal than the average American.

But what's really interesting about this is that, when it comes to religion, there's no more ardent supporters of the Democratic Party than Black Protestants. It's well known that at least 90 percent of Black Protestants cast their ballots for the Democratic nominees at the congressional or presidential level. But here's what most people miss when talking about Black Protestants: they are absolutely not ideologically liberal. In fact, they often describe themselves as political moderates. But before I dig into that myth, a quick discussion of how researchers classify Protestant Christians.

For the past twenty years, academics have embraced a system of religious classification that sorts American Protestant Christians into three distinct groups. Evangelicals are very well known by the average American—theologically and politically conservative. The majority of evangelicals are white; however, the number of evangelicals of color is growing every year as the demographics of the United States are changing. Mainline Protestants represent a more moderate type of Protestant Christianity. They are members of United Methodist, Lutheran, Presbyterian, Episcopal, and other traditions that tend to not see the Bible as literally true but instead should be interpreted in light of modern society. These traditions are overwhelmingly white and tend to be a bit older and more highly educated than evangelicals. However, the third group consists of members of historically Black Protestant traditions. Black Protestants typically come from the charismatic movement inside Protestant Christianity, with the African Methodist Episcopal Church and the Church of God in Christ traditions typifying the Black Protestant tradition.

Distinguishing between evangelicals and Black Protestants has a long historical justification. As Martin Luther King, Jr. famously stated, "the most segregated hour of Christian America is eleven o'clock on Sunday morning." Even after slavery was ended in the United States, it was still not culturally acceptable for African Americans to attend worship with other white Christians, and thus they developed their own approach to Protestant worship. Anyone who has attended worship services in a predominantly white congregation and then a predominantly Black one can quickly attest that the services are vastly different in structure and style. Black churches will often have politicians give speeches from behind the pulpit, something that would be considered anathema to most white Protestants. But that custom is traced back to the fact that Black politicians often had no other platform to drum up support in the Jim Crow era, while their white counterparts were invited to give speeches in a variety of forums throughout the community. This is just one example of how the theological and political culture of Black churches evolved in an entirely different way from white Protestant Christianity.

The most obvious manifestation of this divide between white evangelicalism and historically Black Protestants is at the ballot box. It's been well documented that the religious group that offered Donald Trump the strongest support in November 2020 was white evangelical Protestants. Just over 80 percent of them cast a ballot for Trump during his reelection campaign, while only 18 percent of white evangelicals supported Joe Biden. On the other hand, among Black Protestants just 9 percent backed Trump's reelection bid, while 90 percent were backers of Joe Biden. On election day, it's hard to find two groups more different than Black Protestants and white evangelicals. Thus, it would be easy to assume that Black Protestants are liberals and white evangelicals are conservative. But the data tells a much different story.

The 2020 Cooperative Election Study asked, "Generally speaking, do you think of yourself as a Democrat, Republican, or Independent" as well as asking, "In general, how would you describe your own political viewpoint?" with options ranging from "very liberal" to "very conservative." The distributions of responses to both those questions for Black Protestants are illustrated in figure 17.1.

Given that about nine in ten Black Protestants voted for Joe Biden in 2020, it makes sense that the vast majority of them would affiliate with the Democratic Party. In this case, 82 percent of Black Protestants align with the Democrats, while about 10 percent see themselves as politically independent, and the remaining 8 percent say they are Republicans. However, that same lopsided

Partisanship of Black Protestants

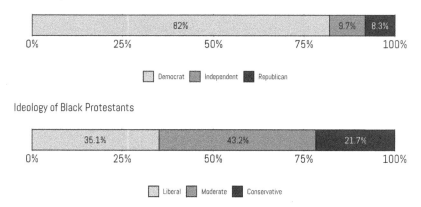

Figure 17.1. Partisanship of Black Protestants and Ideology of Black Protestants

Data from Cooperative Election Study. Stephen Ansolabehere, Brian F. Schaffner, and Sam Luks, Cambridge, MA: Harvard University, http://cces.gov.harvard.edu

distribution is not evident when political ideology is examined. Just 35 percent of Black Protestants describe their ideology as "liberal," which is not that much larger than the share describing themselves as "conservative." The most common response among Black Protestants is "moderate," which encompasses about 43 percent of this religious group. Thus, it's clear from this analysis that for Black Protestants ideology and partisanship are not in alignment.

The positioning of Black Protestants in political space comes into sharper focus when both are viewed in a scatterplot for seventeen different religious groups in the United States. The average partisanship for each group is illustrated horizontally, while the average ideology is displayed on the vertical axis. It quickly becomes clear that there is a strong correlation between both measures. Members of groups that tend to see themselves as conservative are more likely to identify as Republicans, with the same being true for liberals and Democrats. However, Black

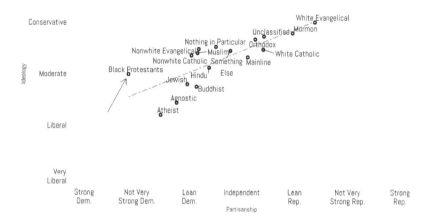

Figure 17.2. Political Positions of Religious Groups

Data from Cooperative Election Study. Stephen Ansolabehere, Brian F. Schaffner, and Sam Luks, Cambridge, MA: Harvard University, http://cces.gov.harvard.edu

Protestants are a true outlier from this linear relationship, as is clear in figure 17.2.

On the horizontal dimension, which is a measure of the average partisanship of each group, no religious group in the United States is more closely aligned with the Democratic Party than Black Protestants. Yet on the vertical dimension, the average Black Protestant identifies as politically moderate, which is about the same position on this scale as Hindus and just slightly more liberal than mainline Protestants. In fact, four religious groups are more ideologically liberal than Black Protestants: Jews, Buddhists, Atheists, and Agnostics. In some ways, atheists are the opposites of Black Protestants. Given the trend line of other religious traditions, we would expect Black Protestants to be significantly more liberal than they are.

When the analytical lens turns to Black Protestants' view of the Bible, there's compelling evidence that the theological difference between the average Black Protestant and a typical evangelical is not that large. The General Social Survey asks respondents about their view of the Bible with three response options: the Bible is the word of God and should be taken literally, the Bible was inspired by God but should not be taken literally, or the Bible is an ancient book of fables.

When biblical literalism is looked at over the last four decades, as in figure 17.3, it's safe to conclude that it is just as prevalent in the Black Protestant tradition as it is among evangelicals. In the 1980s, the share of each tradition that took a literalist position was about 60 percent. In the 1990s and 2000s, the data indicates Black Protestants were actually more likely to believe the Bible

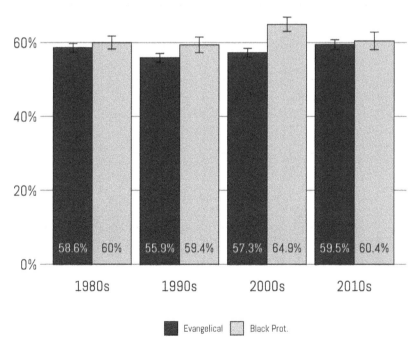

Figure 17.3. Share Who Believe the Bible is Literally True

Data from the General Social Survey, a project of the independent research organization NORC at the University of Chicago, with principal funding from the National Science Foundation, https://gss.norc.org/Get-The-Data

should be taken literally than their evangelical counterparts. In the 2000s, a literalist view was held by 65 percent of Black Protestants, but only by 57 percent of evangelicals. By the 2010s, the share of literalists in each tradition was almost exactly what it was four decades earlier.

When the views of evangelicals and Black Protestants on social issues are analyzed, some daylight does appear between the two groups, however. That's clear in figure 17.4. When it comes to the topic of same-sex marriage, both groups in 2004 opposed the idea, with just 12 percent of evangelicals and 14 percent of Black Protestants expressing support. However, both groups have become more permissive over time, although at slightly different rates. In 2018, 54 percent of Black Protestants supported same-sex marriage compared to 45 percent of evangelicals.

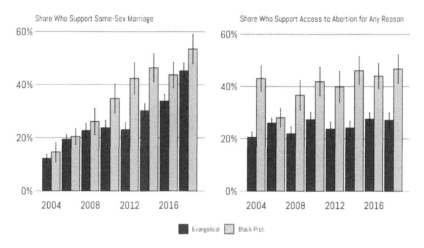

Figure 17.4. View of Social Issues among Evangelicals and Black Protestants

Data from the General Social Survey, a project of the independent research organization NORC at the University of Chicago, with principal funding from the National Science Foundation, https://gss.norc.org/Get-The-Data

In terms of allowing access to abortion for any reason, we see a great deal more stability in the data from 2004 through 2018. In a typical year, about 40 percent of Black Protestants support access to abortion, while the figure is lower for evangelicals, at around 25 percent. When looked at broadly, there is some evidence that Black Protestants are not as conservative as their evangelical contemporaries. However, that does not mean that Black Protestants are social liberals. Consider that until 2018, the majority of Black Protestants did not support same-sex marriage and a majority of Black Protestants do not support access to abortion for any reason in any year in the data. So while they are to the left of evangelicals, they are clearly still much more conservative than other Democrats on these measures.

CONCLUSIONS

Black Protestants represent an interesting prism through which to view the current relationship between religion and politics in the United States. There is no more politically unified religious voting bloc in contemporary American politics than Black Protestants. At least nine in ten of them can be expected to vote for the Democratic nominee in the next presidential election. While many political commentators love to mention the fact that white evangelicals have an incredibly tight bond with the Republican Party, they are still more politically diverse than Black Protestants, as about 20 percent of them voted for Joe Biden in the 2020 presidential election.

Yet it still seems that the Democratic Party has an uneasy relationship with religiously devout and socially conservative Black Protestants. I am always amazed that the Democratic coalition consists of Black Protestants on one side and atheists on the other. While both groups can find common ground on things like economic and racial policy, they could not be more different when it comes to other social issues.

In many ways, it seems like the flaws in the American two-party system come into clear focus when considering the position of Black Protestants. It's not far-fetched to assume that many Black Protestants would welcome an alternative political party that was conservative on issues such as abortion and gay marriage but supported more progressive economic and racial policy. But because of the structure of our electoral system, this religious group is stuck with choosing between two candidates who don't represent their complete range of views.

There's ample evidence that political parties are always trying to find ways to win over new groups of voters in each subsequent election. Donald Trump made several appeals to Black voters in the 2020 campaign but was unsuccessful in moving that voting bloc in a significant way. It may be the case that as the size of the religiously unaffiliated continues to rise each year, the Democratic Party may have to cater to this growing group, which could alienate more religiously devout parts of their coalition. So while Black Protestants do vote in huge numbers for Democrats, their moderate positions on social policy may make them a potential target for outreach by some Republicans in the years to come.

For Further Reading

McDaniel, Eric L. *Politics in the Pews: The Political Mobilization of Black Churches*. Ann Arbor: University of Michigan Press, 2008.

McDaniel keeps a congregation-level view of how politics works in the Black church. He provides a window into how pastors have to be able to network effectively with politicians and government leaders to help their church and their community.

Owens, Michael L. *God and Government in the Ghetto: The Politics of Church-State Collaboration in Black America*. Chicago: University of Chicago Press, 2007.

One of the most important shifts that has occurred with social services in the United States is that government agencies have partnered with faith-based organizations to help local communities more directly. Owens' deep dive on this topic helps to explain how Black pastors use their position to help their communities and their congregations.

Shelton, Jason E., and Michael O. Emerson. *Blacks and Whites in Christian America: How Racial Discrimination Shapes Religious Convictions*. New York: NYU Press, 2012.

This book is the most comprehensive quantitative description of the experience of Black Protestants in print today. Using troves of survey data, Shelton and Emerson paint a nuanced portrait of the beliefs, behaviors, and aspirations of Black churches across the United States.

Mainline Protestants are politically liberal

WHEN SCHOLARS DISCUSS WHITE AMERICAN PROT-
estantism, they usually divide it into two categories: evangelicals
and mainline Protestants. Most people already have a good concept of evangelical churches. They frequently feature praise bands
that lead worshipers in contemporary choruses. They are conservative both theologically and politically. The pastor will often talk
about heaven and hell, judgment, and the need for people to have
a personal relationship with Jesus Christ. These churches do not
affirm those who identify as LGBT. Many are affiliated with the
Southern Baptist Convention or possibly the Assemblies of God,
although, as discussed in myth 6, nondenominational evangelical churches are a growing phenomenon in American religion.

The counterpart to evangelicals is mainline Protestant Christianity. When scholars of religion describe denominations associated with the mainline, the most common term is the "Seven
Sisters of American Protestantism." Those denominations include
the United Methodist Church, the Evangelical Lutheran Church in
America, the Presbyterian Church (U.S.A.), the Episcopal Church,
the American Baptist Church, the United Church of Christ, and the
Disciples of Christ. While the worship style of mainline churches
tends to vary, it's fair to say that many mainline traditions look
more like Catholic worship, with more ornate worship spaces and

with the pastor and other worship leaders sometimes wearing special robes to conduct the worship service. The pastors of these congregations can be men or women, but the sermons are often shorter and don't focus so much on topics like judgment and damnation. Instead, mainline pastors tend to focus on themes such as love, forgiveness, and racial/economic justice. As can likely be ascertained from this description, these types of churches are not as theologically conservative as their evangelical counterparts.

For many evangelicals, mainline Christian traditions are often held up as examples of what churches should not be. For instance, Dave Shifflet's 2005 book, *Exodus: Why Americans Are Fleeing*

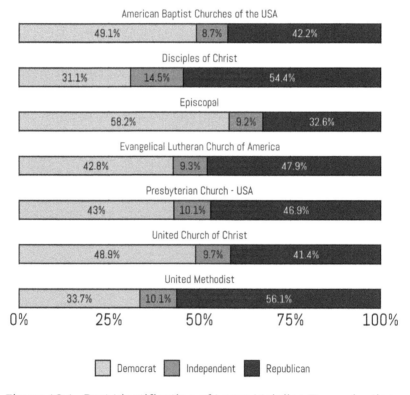

Figure 18.1. Part Identification of Large Mainline Denominations

Data from Cooperative Election Study. Stephen Ansolabehere, Brian F. Schaffner, and Sam Luks, Cambridge, MA: Harvard University, http://cces.gov.harvard.edu

Liberal Churches for Conservative Christianity, argues that the only type of religion that has staying power is conservative religion. Evangelicals often misperceive their mainline cousins. They assume that because they are not as conservative (theologically or politically) as they are, they must be liberal. However, the data tells a different story. There's no real evidence to indicate that the average mainline Protestant church is filled with large numbers of Democratic voters. In fact, a number of mainline traditions (namely the United Methodist Church) could be described as politically right of center. Figure 18.1 assesses the partisanship of the Seven Sisters, which gives us a window into the partisanship of the mainline tradition.

A glance at figure 18.2 reveals that many of these denominations could be described as politically diverse. For instance, about 49 percent of American Baptists are Democrats, while 42 percent are Republicans—a fairly well-balanced distribution of political views. That same mix also shows up among PCUSA and UCC members. The only tradition of these seven in which it's fair to say Democrats outnumber Republicans by a wide margin is the Episcopal church, where 58 percent are Democrats and just 33 percent are Republicans, a twenty-five-point spread. But in the largest of all the mainline denominations—the United Methodist Church—the Republicans outnumber the Democrats by over twenty-two percentage points.

Thus, there's little evidence here to make the claim that mainline Protestants are politically liberal. In only one tradition do Democrats clearly make up at least half of the congregation. In many cases the gap between Republicans and Democrats is less than ten percentage points. A more accurate statement is that mainline churches are not politically homogeneous. That political diversity comes into sharper focus when comparing mainline denominations against some of the larger traditions in American evangelicalism.

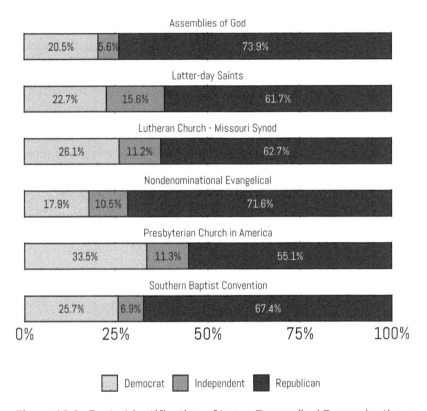

Figure 18.2. Party Identification of Large Evangelical Denominations
Data from Cooperative Election Study. Stephen Ansolabehere, Brian F. Schaffner, and Sam Luks, Cambridge, MA: Harvard University, http://cces.gov.harvard.edu

The largest Protestant denomination in the United States is the Southern Baptist Convention. In that tradition, over two-thirds of all members identify with the Republican party while just a quarter align themselves with the Democrats. For the SBC, the partisan gap is more than forty percentage points. Among nondenominational evangelicals, there's an even larger gap. Almost 72 percent of nondenominationals say they are Republicans, compared to only 18 percent who are Democrats—a gap of fifty-four points. The gap for Lutherans in the Missouri Synod is thirty-six percentage points, and in the Assemblies of God it's fifty-three points. In other words, all these traditions are overwhelmingly Republican. The most politically diverse evangelical denomination is the Presbyterian Church in America, where the partisan gap is still twenty-two points.

Recall that in only one mainline tradition do the Democrats outnumber the Republicans by at least twenty percentage points. In all six of the evangelical traditions analyzed here, the Republicans outnumber the Democrats by at least twenty-two percentage points. There's no tradition in the mainline that's as politically homogeneous as the Southern Baptist Convention or the Assemblies of God. If the sample were restricted to just white evangelicals in these denominations, the percentages would be even more lopsided for the Republicans.

Looked at holistically, there's ample evidence to claim that evangelical Protestant Christianity is overwhelmingly aligned with the Republican party, as discussed in myth 18. In many of these traditions Republicans outnumber Democrats by a three-to-one margin. But for the mainline, there's a lot more political diversity. In the average mainline church, Republicans and Democrats can be found in nearly equal numbers.

That said, this data comes from surveys conducted in 2020. The myth that mainline Protestants are liberals may have some empirical support when comparing the political partisanship of mainline and evangelical Protestants twenty or thirty years ago. Using the General Social Survey, I calculated the share of white mainline Protestants who identified as Republicans compared to white evangelicals dating back to 1972. Restricting the sample to just white respondents is necessary, because mainline traditions tend to be less racially diverse than their evangelical counterparts. The results of that analysis provide a fascinating look into how the perception of the political landscape can shift over time based on the relative movement of other religious groups.

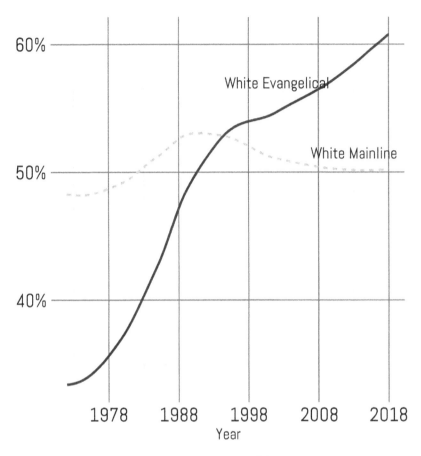

Figure 18.3. Share Identifying as Republican

Data from the General Social Survey, a project of the independent research organization NORC at the University of Chicago, with principal funding from the National Science Foundation, https://gss.norc.org/Get-The-Data

As is shown in figure 18.3, in the early 1970s, there was a tremendous partisan gap between white evangelical Protestants and white mainline Protestants. Just under 50 percent of mainliners affiliated with the Republican party in 1975 compared to only a third of white evangelicals. Consider that for a second—throughout most of the 1970s, fewer than 35 percent of white evangelicals were Republicans, while just under half of mainline Protestants were. However, things quickly began to change for evangelicals.

By 1983, about 40 percent of white evangelicals aligned with the GOP. That share rose a full ten percentage points in the next eight years, when a majority of white evangelicals aligned with the Republican party for the first time. That share reached 55 percent by 2003 and then went beyond 60 percent in 2016. While evangelicals made a dramatic shift in their partisan loyalties during that forty-five-year span, white mainline Protestants were much less volatile. After becoming 5 percent more Republican between 1972 and 1990, white mainline Protestants slowly drifted away from the Republican party. By 2018, about half of them aligned with the GOP, which is not statistically different from the share who were Republicans back in the 1970s.

Consider how political commentators would have described American Protestants in both the 1970s and today. Four decades ago, it would have been statistically justifiable to describe white evangelicals as a key voting bloc in the Democratic coalition. A third of them aligned with the Republican Party (while about half of mainline Protestants were attached to the GOP). However, a pundit could look at the data from the past decade and say that mainline Protestants are clearly to the left of white evangelicals based on the share of each who identify with a political party, and they are justified in that declaration. When someone is asked if they are politically liberal or conservative, it seems entirely reasonable to respond to that query with a question: "Compared to what?"

Mainline Protestants today are more liberal than their evangelical counterparts, but that's only a result of the continued rightward drift of the evangelical tradition—not because mainline Protestants have shifted hard to the left but because when it comes to political partisanship, the definition of terms like "conservative" and "liberal" is always drifting. For instance,

George W. Bush was seen as very conservative when he was in the White House, but now many of the loudest voices in the GOP see him as ideologically moderate. When evangelicals say mainline Protestants are liberals, they are falling victim to a type of cognitive bias called an "anchoring error." Human beings are constantly evaluating things against reference points. Those reference points (or anchors) help us to place other people and groups in social space. For evangelicals, their anchoring point is themselves. Thus, anyone who is less conservative than they are is liberal. However, if their anchor point were the average

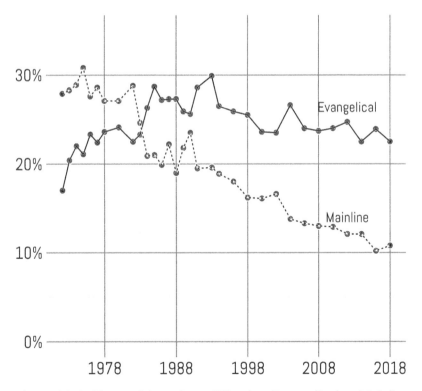

Figure 18.4. Share of Americans Who Are Evangelical or Mainline

Data from the General Social Survey, a project of the independent research organization NORC at the University of Chicago, with principal funding from the National Science Foundation, https://gss.norc.org/Get-The-Data

American, they would see mainline Protestants as being slightly to the right of center.

However, this discussion needs to be contextualized, because the size of evangelicals has shifted in comparison to those who are mainline Protestants, as shown in figure 18.4. As discussed in myth 1, the share of Americans who identify as evangelicals is at least as large today as it was four decades ago. On the other hand, mainline Protestants have seen an entirely different trajectory. In 1975, over 30 percent of all Americans were affiliated with a mainline Protestant tradition. That was nearly ten points higher than the share of Americans who were evangelicals. But things began to decline for the mainline tradition from that point forward. By 1988, just 20 percent of all Americans identified as a mainline Protestant. That share was cut in half by 2016, when just about one in ten Americans were mainline Protestants. In 2018, the share of Americans who were evangelicals was double the size of those who were mainline Protestants.

CONCLUSIONS

So if mainline Protestants worship at churches that tend to be more open to women in leadership roles and are affirming of LGBT individuals, why do they not appear as more politically liberal than the data indicates? The reason lies largely in factors that are beyond the culture war issues that were discussed in myth 12. Historically, mainline Protestant churches were often filled with members who came from white-collar professions in the local community. Doctors, lawyers, and small business owners would often attend the United Methodist Church or Episcopal church in town. Because of their educational background and occupation, many families in the mainline had above-average incomes, and for many, this became the most important factor when it came to deciding who to vote for on election day.

I have heard more than one scholar of American religion say that a mainline Protestant is a specific type of voter, "a country club Republican." These individuals are not activated by topics like gay marriage or abortion. In fact, many of them take a more libertarian position on social issues: the government should let people have freedom to do what they see fit. However, that laissez-faire approach also extends to issues of taxing and government spending. They don't want to pay high taxes, and they don't want lots of rules and regulations governing their businesses and other aspects of their lives.

In my mind, George H. W. Bush typifies this approach to politics. A lifelong Episcopalian, Bush steered clear of the influences of the religious right as much as possible when he ran for the presidency in 1988 and 1992. It's fair to say that he was a moderate on social issues. In fact, in 2013, he attended a same-sex wedding ceremony in Maine. However, Republicans like him are nearly extinct in the American political landscape. That puts mainline Protestants in a truly difficult position when it comes to election day. While many of them approve of smaller government, they abhor the GOP's policies on things like immigration and the rights of LGBT Americans. At the same time, the Democratic party is becoming less Christian and more secular as each year passes. When a topic like religious freedom emerges, many mainline Protestants want the government to allow churches to behave in ways that comport to their church doctrine, while atheists and agnostics do not share the same policy views. In many ways, the significant political polarization facing the United States has hit mainline Protestants the hardest, making many of them feel like they are politically homeless. Unfortunately, because of the declining size and influence of the mainline, it seems that neither party is particularly focused on reaching out to this religious tradition, which means the mainline will likely feel politically adrift for the foreseeable future.

For Further Reading

Findlay, James F. *Church People in the Struggle: the National Council of Churches and the Black Freedom Movement, 1950–1970*. Oxford University Press on Demand, 1993.

The National Council of Churches was once the most important religious organization in the United States. Made up primarily of churches in the mainline tradition, it partnered with many Black churches in the South to fight for Civil Rights. This book does a tremendous job of describing some of the successes and failures of that collaboration.

Jones, Robert P. *The End of White Christian America*. New York: Simon and Schuster, 2016.

Robert Jones is the CEO of the Public Religion Research Institute, an organization that does extensive polling on politics and religion among the American public. His 2016 book lays out, in stark detail, how white Christianity is declining rapidly in both size and influence.

Roof, Wade Clark, and William McKinney. *American Mainline Religion: Its Changing Shape and Future*. New Brunswick, NJ: Rutgers University Press, 1987.

While this book is a bit older, there's tremendous value in reading this volume from Roof and McKinney because they describe the mainline when it was still a dominant force in American political and religious life. The authors also begin to map the contours of American evangelicalism, which was reaching its peak.

Young evangelicals are more politically moderate than older evangelicals

IT'S A STORY THAT I SEE POP UP IN A MAJOR MEDIA outlet from time to time. An article ran in *Time* magazine in 2015 with the headline "Why the Young Religious Right Is Leaning Left,"[35] and the *New Yorker* ran a longer piece in 2018 entitled "Millennial Evangelicals Diverge from Their Parents' Beliefs."[36] Both authors are circling around the same point—that younger evangelicals are breaking away from the tradition of their parents. They paint a picture of younger evangelicals who are not so wed to the Republican Party, who are concerned with a variety of social and racial issues, and who are especially focused on policies surrounding the environment.

I completely understand the urge to write these stories. Having spoken with dozens of religion reporters over the past few years, I have heard from many of them that they (and their audiences) are tired of reading the same old stories about evangelicals over and over again. It's really hard to write "Evangelicals are very conservative Republicans" with a new spin after every election cycle. So reporters and others are always seeking a way to put a different spin on that narrative. An obvious place to look is among the youngest evangelicals.

For instance, the story from the *New Yorker* is centered around the young congregants of the Block Church, an evangelical church plant located in Center City, Philadelphia. It describes an evangelical community that has large contingents of white, Black, and Latino members. However, the author also correctly notes that according to data from the National Congregations Study, 86 percent of evangelical churches are racially segregated. Thus, the main characters of the piece do not accurately reflect the typical evangelical church.

The thesis of pieces like this is that young evangelicals are at least thinking carefully about their electoral choices and that the connection between their faith and their attachment to conservative politics and the Republican party is not as strong as it is for their evangelical parents or grandparents. But a careful look at the data indicates that by almost any measure, young white evangelicals are consistently conservative and vote in overwhelming numbers for the Republican candidate for president. Additionally, there's not much evidence that their views on abortion or the environment have moderated in any meaningful way from young white evangelicals ten or twenty years ago. In short, there's not much hope that the union between evangelicalism and Republicanism will weaken at any point in the near future.

Before digging into the political views of young evangelicals, it's important to understand how their share of the population has changed over time. Figure 19.1 displays the percentage of eighteen- to thirty-five-year-olds of any race and whites who were evangelicals. In the early 1970s, about 20 percent of young people identified as evangelical (regardless of race), but that share grew steadily through the 1980s. By 1990, about 26 percent of all young people were evangelical, while about 22 percent of young whites were evangelicals. Those shares began to decline from that point forward. By 2008, only 21 percent of young Americans of

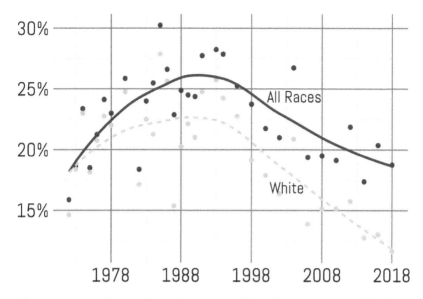

Figure 19.1. Share of 18-35-Year-Olds Who Are Evangelical

Data from the General Social Survey, a project of the independent research organization NORC at the University of Chicago, with principal funding from the National Science Foundation, https://gss.norc.org/Get-The-Data

any race were evangelical, and just 16 percent of young whites were evangelicals. That decline has only accelerated among white evangelicals, as only 13 percent of white Americans between the ages of eighteen and thirty-five identify as evangelical today. That's the lowest percentage in the forty-six-year history of the General Social Survey.

But has that change in size led to a shift in their political views? A good way to view this bond between the Republican party and young white evangelicals is through the lens of political partisanship. When white evangelicals are broken down into five age groups, as was done for figure 19.2, we do not see a lot of differences in their partisan makeup. For those between the ages of 18 and 35, 56 percent align with the Republican party, while, politically, 30 percent are Independents and just 15 percent are

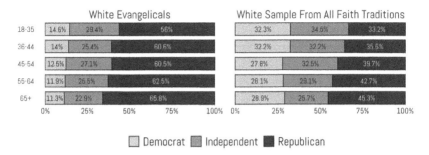

Figure 19.2. Political Partisanship by Age

Data from Cooperative Election Study. Stephen Ansolabehere, Brian F. Schaffner, and Sam Luks, Cambridge, MA: Harvard University, http://cces.gov.harvard.edu

Democrats. In the sample of white eighteen- to thirty-five-year-olds of all faith traditions, there's almost an even distribution, with about a third saying that they are Democrats, another third indicating they are Republicans, and the remaining portion being political Independents. In other words, a young white evangelical is about twenty-three points more likely to be a Republican than other young white people.

Looking at both graphs, it becomes quickly apparent that the likelihood of identifying as politically independent is highest among the youngest Americans, and that propensity decreases as people age. In essence, older Americans are more inclined to pick a side in the partisan battle. In the case of young white evangelicals, nearly three in ten indicate that they are politically independent. Yet, in most presidential elections, there are not a lot of options on the ballot for those who don't align with either political party. Presidential elections are times when people are almost forced to choose either the Republican or the Democrat. Because of the winner-take-all system of American elections, there's little incentive to vote for a third-party candidate. The data is clear on this: young white evangelicals favor the Republican by a significant margin.

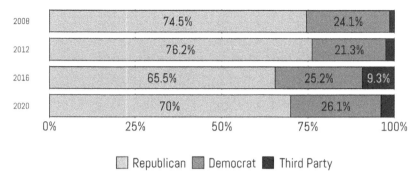

Figure 19.3. Vote for President among White Evangelicals, 18–39 Years Old

Data from Cooperative Election Study. Stephen Ansolabehere, Brian F. Schaffner, and Sam Luks, Cambridge, MA: Harvard University, http://cces.gov.harvard.edu

Looking across the past four election cycles in figure 19.3,[37] there's clear evidence that when it comes time to vote, young white evangelicals look more similar to their evangelical parents and grandparents than they do to other young people. In Barack Obama's election in 2008, he earned less than one-quarter of the young white evangelical vote. John McCain garnered about three-quarters. That doesn't deviate in any meaningful way from the vote distribution of all white evangelicals in 2008. The 2012 election was essentially a repeat of the 2008 race, although Mitt Romney did just a bit better than McCain, while Obama lost some ground in his reelection bid.

The 2016 election between Donald Trump and Hillary Clinton does look like a bit of an aberration compared to the prior two contests. Trump received about two-thirds of the votes of young white evangelicals, while Hillary Clinton's share was just about a quarter. In the 2008 and 2012 elections, the Republican garnered three-quarters of the young white evangelical vote. A fair number of third-party votes—9 percent—were cast by white evangelicals between the ages of 18 and 35. It seems reasonable to use this as evidence that the GOP's grip on the young white evangelical vote was fading. However, the results from 2020 cast some doubt on that claim. The share of third-party voters dropped from 9 percent to just 4 percent, almost all of that shift the result of young white evangelicals throwing their support behind Trump's reelection bid. The incumbent Republican did nearly five points better in 2020 compared to 2016, while Biden may have gained only one point over Clinton's total four years earlier.

Looked at in totality, it does seem fair to conclude that young white evangelicals initially expressed less affinity for Donald Trump (as a larger portion voted for the third-party candidates) compared to John McCain or Mitt Romney. However, that shift is tempered by the fact that Trump still got 70 percent of this voting bloc in 2020, only five points less than McCain in 2008. On the other hand, there's very little evidence to indicate that young white evangelicals are willing to support a Democratic candidate. Joe Biden did just two points better in 2020 than Barack Obama in 2008. If there's evidence of young white evangelicals defecting from the GOP, it doesn't show up in the voting data.

If we focus on policy issues, it quickly becomes apparent why young white evangelicals have not shifted their voting patterns in any significant way in recent years, as can be seen in figure 19.4. The General Social Survey has been asking questions about a number of policy areas, including abortion and the environment, since its inception in the early 1970s. Thus, it's possible for us to assess whether the young white evangelicals of the 2010s have different policy views compared with younger evangelicals in the 1970s and 1980s.

When it comes to allowing access to an abortion for any reason, about 30 percent of white evangelicals between the ages of 18 and 35 supported the possibility through the 1980s and into the early 1990s. Then support for access to abortion dropped precipitously over the next fifteen years. In the 2000s, it hit a low point, with

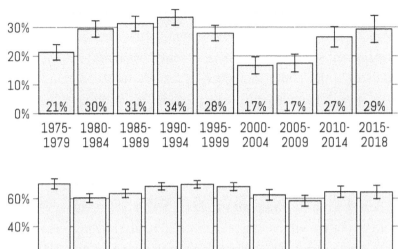

Figure 19.4. Share Supporting Access to Abortion for Any Reason among White Evangelicals, 18–35 Years Old Share Saying We Are Spending Too Little on Protecting the Environment among White Evangelicals, 18–35 Years Old

Data from the General Social Survey, a project of the independent research organization NORC at the University of Chicago, with principal funding from the National Science Foundation, https://gss.norc.org/Get-The-Data

only 17 percent of young white evangelicals supporting access to abortion for any reason. Since then, support for a woman's right to choose has climbed to about 30 percent of young white evangelicals, which is not statistically different from opinions about abortion in the 1980s.

Views about environmentalism have been relatively stable. The GSS asked respondents if the federal government was spending too much, too little, or about the right amount on improving and protecting the environment. Significant majorities of young white evangelicals have been saying too little for the better part of the past four decades. Through the 1970s and 1980s, about 70 percent of young white evangelicals believed that the government should spend more on environmental causes. That did drop in the 2000s, however, to just about 60 percent. Since then, there's been a small rebound, and it would be fair to say about two-thirds of white evangelicals between the ages of 18 and 35 think that the government should spend more on protecting the environment. That's slightly lower than the results from the 1990s.

Based on these two policy issues, there's little evidence to say that the young white evangelicals of 2020 are any less conservative than young white evangelicals of a few decades ago. The level of support for abortion among this group is no different today than it was among the young white evangelicals of three decades ago, and there's some evidence that they are less supportive of spending money on environmental protection than young white evangelicals from the 1990s. However, there is one issue about which young white evangelicals have clearly moved in a more progressive direction: same-sex marriage.

The first time that the General Social Survey asked about marriage between people of the same sex was in 1988. While 14 percent of all respondents between the ages of 18 and 35 supported the idea, only 3 percent of young white evangelicals did, as can be seen in figure 19.5. The question wasn't asked again until 2004, when 43 percent of all young people were in favor compared to just 20 percent of young white evangelicals. But from that point forward, support among both groups began to rise very rapidly. In 2018, 79 percent of young people supported same-sex marriage compared to 56 percent of young white evangelicals. Given the fact that opinion on this issue has shifted so rapidly, it would be fair to assume that at least 60 percent of white evangelicals between the ages of 18 and 35 are in favor of same-sex unions today. That's an increase of nearly 60 percent in just over

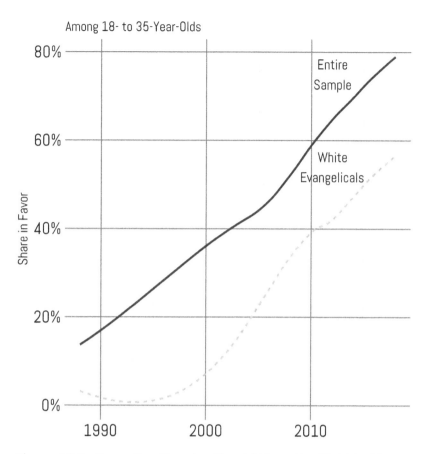

Figure 19.5. Same-Sex Couples Should Have the Right to Marry: Among 18- to 35-Year-Olds

three decades. However, it's worth pointing out that young white evangelicals still lag behind young people by nearly twenty-five percentage points on this question.

CONCLUSIONS

One of the most widely understood relationships in American politics is between age and partisanship. On average, younger people tend to be more liberal in their political views, while older

Americans are more conservative. It's always been a bit more difficult for a young person to be politically conservative than their parents or grandparents, because they feel a great deal of pressure to conform to the views of their peers. For many young people who saw themselves as conservative evangelicals, the past two decades have created a social and political gauntlet that they have had to navigate. The share of young people who have publicly declared that they are gay, lesbian, bisexual, or transgender has risen dramatically in the last few years. At the same time, the United States has become more racially and ethnically diverse than ever before. Young people have friends and classmates from a variety of faith traditions and countries of origin. The current iteration of the Republican party has focused on promoting bills that discriminate against transgender students and made it more difficult to legally immigrate to the United States. Defending those policies is difficult when people are surrounded by many of their peers who are negatively impacted by those policies. Thus, those young people who still choose to identify as evangelical do so because they are true believers in the doctrines, politics, and policies of that religious tradition.

From this angle, it makes sense that the polling data indicates young evangelicals are just as conservative as that same group two or three decades earlier. What is worrisome about this situation from a purely democratic perspective is that young people who are evangelical and those who are not have moved even further apart when it comes to views of society, morality, and ideology, inevitably making it harder to build bridges between them. Political polarization makes governing by consensus much more difficult, but the future of the American form of government seems downright untenable when considering the distance between these two groups of young people. Democracy relies on compromise, which becomes impossible if one side sees the other as the enemy.

Winning people over to their faith is a crucial part of evangelical religious identity, though evangelicals also often pride themselves on behaving differently from the rest of society. However, winning people for Christ becomes severely impaired and behaving differently may come at a large cost if there's little commonality between young evangelicals and other young people. Even young people who are interested in Christianity may be turned off by the fact that the loudest voices preaching the Gospel in their generation are those from the most conservative tradition in American Protestantism. Some who may have been open to hearing the message of Jesus Christ will not be if it is entangled with what they view as a set of homophobic and xenophobic political positions. This polarization imperils the future of American politics, society, and religion.

For Further Reading

Castle, Jeremiah. *Rock of Ages:Subcultural Religious Identity and Public Opinion among Young Evangelicals*. Philadelphia, PA: Temple University Press, 2019.

Castle looks at the political worldview of young evangelicals using a variety of data sources. He illuminates two areas—same-sex marriage and the environment—where young evangelicals may influence the views of the Republican Party.

Kinnaman, David, and Gabe Lyons. *unChristian: What a New Generation Really Thinks About Christianity... and Why it Matters*. Ada, MI: Baker Books, 2007.

David Kinnaman is the president of the Barna research group, one of the most important survey firms in American evangelicalism. His book with Gabe Lyons is data driven and practical. The authors delineate six problematic areas of evangelical behavior. They also advise how the church can do a better job of reaching out to young people.

Smith, Buster G., and Byron Johnson. "The Liberalization of Young Evangelicals: A Research Note." *Journal for the Scientific Study of Religion* 49, no. 2 (2010): 351–60.

This short article by Smith and Johnson was published while I was in graduate school and was instrumental in helping me think through the worldview of young evangelicals. Their initial findings are largely in line with other work in this field: young evangelicals are conservative on some social issues but are open to environmental protection.

Pastors often discuss politics from the pulpit

IN THE SUMMER OF 1954, A YOUNG SENATOR FROM Texas named Lyndon B. Johnson proposed an amendment to the Internal Revenue Code of 1954 that was winding its way through Congress. At the time, the change was largely seen as being innocuous. Johnson wanted a provision inserted into the tax code that prohibited nonprofits (those classified as 501(c)(3) organizations) from engaging in explicitly political acts, such as officially endorsing a candidate or fundraising for a political party. Johnson's logic was simple: if nonprofits were going to be insulated from paying most kinds of taxes, they should also be prohibited from engaging in political activity. If an organization violated that provision, the IRS was empowered to revoke their tax-exempt status and begin levying taxes. The provision was seen as so noncontroversial that it's almost impossible to find any mention of the provision in news coverage when it was adopted. In 1986, the Reagan administration worked with Congress to significantly overhaul the tax structure of the United States and this provision was left unchanged. Policymakers viewed this provision as legally necessary and apolitical.[38]

In the past three decades, that clause in the American tax code began to be referred to as the Johnson Amendment, and references to it increasingly began to appear in campaign speeches and political talk radio. Political liberals have been quick to point out video or audio clips posted online of sermons in which the pastor would explicitly endorse a candidate for political office as evidence of conservative churches flouting the law. At the same time, political conservatives have decried the Johnson Amendment as a fundamental attack on the First Amendment's protection of free speech. Their argument is that pastors should not lose their constitutional rights when they enter the pulpit on Sunday morning.

A number of high-profile skirmishes over the Johnson Amendment have occurred in just the past few years. In 2008, the conservative Christian advocacy group Alliance Defending Freedom established an annual event called "Pulpit Freedom Sunday." On the Sunday following April 15 (the date individual income tax filings are due), pastors are encouraged to make statements during their sermon that specifically violate the Johnson Amendment's prohibition against political endorsements. When the event was launched, thirty-three pastors took part, not only making political statements but also mailing recordings of their Sunday sermon to the IRS in hopes of having their tax-exempt status revoked and leading to a court challenge to the Johnson Amendment. To date, no church has lost its tax exemption for participating in Pulpit Freedom Sunday.

During his campaign for president in 2016, Donald Trump often referred to the Johnson Amendment during rallies and speeches to Christian groups. He promised his supporters that if elected, he would have the amendment struck from the tax code. In 2019, at the National Day of Prayer service he stated, "We got rid of the Johnson Amendment."[39] In actuality, the president had signed an executive order in 2017 that did give more latitude to churches when it comes to political speech but did not fundamentally alter the prohibitions of the amendment.

But for all the attempts to usher in the demise of the Johnson Amendment, giving pastors free rein to speak about whatever topics they choose and endorse whichever candidates they see fit, there's not much empirical support for the claim that pastors are regularly engaging in political rhetoric from the pulpit. In fact, numerous studies have concluded that people in the pews rarely hear political messaging during the Sunday sermon. Thus, most of the fight surrounding the Johnson Amendment is symbolic and would likely have little to no impact on the political climate of churches across the United States.

In the spring of 2019, my frequent collaborator Paul Djupe and I received a generous grant from the Louisville Institute to field a survey that was focused on understanding the political, social, and spiritual world of Protestant Christians in the United States. Half the sample came from denominational Protestant traditions such as Baptists, Methodists, and Presbyterians. The other half was drawn from those who identified with a nondenominational church. We asked respondents if they had heard their pastor address ten different political topics in the prior year, and the results indicate that political speech from the pulpit is infrequent.

As figure 20.1 indicates, 30 percent of respondents indicated that they had not heard their pastor discuss politics at all. That's the same percentage as those who indicated that their pastor had discussed religious freedom. Additionally, a quarter of respondents said they had heard their pastor address abortion from the pulpit, with basically the same share noting they had heard their pastor speak about poverty and gay rights during the weekend message.

Just 16 percent of respondents said that they had heard their pastor even discuss Donald Trump in the prior twelve months. Fewer than one in ten Protestant Christians could recall a time in the previous year when their pastor touched on topics related to healthcare, Islam in the United States, and the investigations

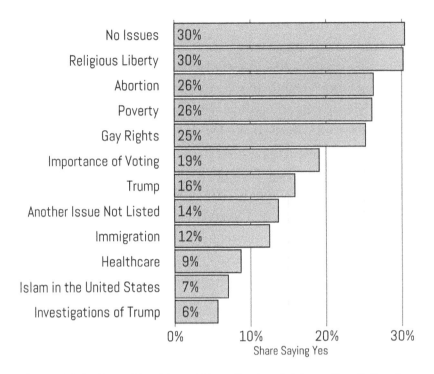

Figure 20.1. Have You Heard Your Pastor Address the Following Topics in the Last Year?

Data from a survey written by Paul Djupe (Denison University) and Ryan Burge and administered through Qualtrics in Fall 2019. The sample was 500 denominational Protestants and 500 nondenominational Protestants and was funded by the Louisville Institute.

of Donald Trump. Thus, there's very little evidence to support the claim that pastors engage in explicit politicking from the pulpit. If anything, the reverse seems to be true—the vast majority of sermons are devoid of political discussion.

To drive that point home even further, I created an additive index, which gave each respondent a point for each issue they reported they had heard addressed from the pulpit in the prior year. This appears in figure 20.2. According to this sample, over half of respondents (55 percent) indicated they had heard either

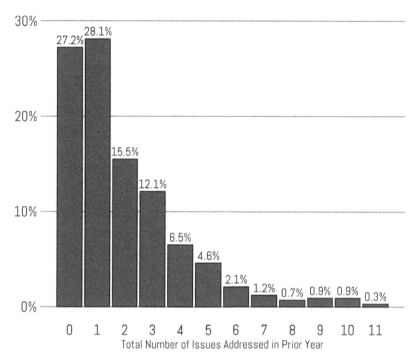

Figure 20.2. Number of Issues Heard during Sermons in Past Year

Data from a survey written by Paul Djupe (Denison University) and Ryan Burge and administered through Qualtrics in Fall 2019. The sample was 500 denominational Protestants and 500 nondenominational Protestants and was funded by the Louisville Institute.

one political issue or no political issues addressed from the pulpit in the prior year. Another 15 percent listed two political issues during the time frame, and 12 percent said that they had heard three issues discussed. Added together, about 83 percent of Protestant Christians said that they had heard three political issues or fewer during Sunday sermons. Just 11 percent said that they had heard more than six political issues mentioned. Thus, it seems prudent to conclude that most churches engage in very little political discussion from the pulpit—with a significant portion of Protestants hearing almost no political discussion from their pastor.

But there's another question that looms behind all of this discussion surrounding the politicization of churches. Does the average churchgoer actually want their church to engage in political discussions and activism? The assumption among many secular liberals is that Christians want their pastor to endorse candidates and to speak explicitly about political matters during weekend messages. To test that, we asked respondents if they wanted their church to keep out of political matters or if they wanted their church leaders to express their views on political questions. We also asked if they wanted their church to provide forums for political discussion or if they wanted them to avoid political discussion entirely. In both cases, respondents were given the option to not take a side on the question.

What we found, illustrated in figure 20.3, was decidedly mixed when it comes to Protestants' views about their church and politics. For instance, on the question of whether churches should engage in politics or keep out of political matters, the share who wanted their churches to be apolitical was statistically the same as the share that wanted their church to be more politically involved.

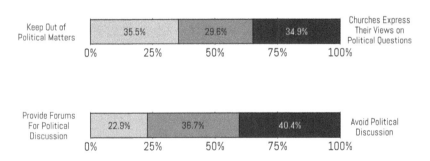

Figure 20.3. Which Comes Closer to Your View of Church

Data from a survey written by Paul Djupe (Denison University) and Ryan Burge and administered through Qualtrics in Fall 2019. The sample was 500 denominational Protestants and 500 nondenominational Protestants and was funded by the Louisville Institute.

Another 30 percent of respondents were undecided on this question. In terms of churches providing forums for political debate, a plurality (40 percent) indicated they would rather their church avoid political discussion, while only about a quarter (23 percent) believed their church should provide a forum for political debate. About 37 percent of respondents did not choose a side on this question.

CONCLUSIONS

Why is there such a large disconnect between the widespread belief that many conservative pastors are extolling the virtues of the Republican party—for example, decrying abortion and same-sex marriage as immoral acts—and the reality that very few pastors are actually talking about politics from the pulpit? Some of it may be due to the types of stories that are often highlighted in the media. A single pastor causing a controversy by being political may get a mention on the nightly news, while thousands of sermons every week that steer far away from political discussion are never mentioned on social media or a news website.

Another possibility may be rooted in the fact that many pastors may be making political points without being overtly political. For instance, it wouldn't be uncommon for a pastor to make a statement like, "Human life is important to God, and therefore human life must be important to Christians." On its face, that statement doesn't seem overtly tied to any political party or candidate. But in fact, the pastor might be making an oblique reference to a number of political issues, including abortion, assisted suicide, the death penalty, or military intervention. Thus, political rhetoric may be happening on a more widespread scale, but it may be occurring so subtly that most people in the pews are just not detecting that their pastor's sermon had political undertones.

If churches are seen as political, however, but the data indicates pastors aren't preaching a lot of politics, then how did millions of white Christians across thousands of churches begin moving toward the conservative side of the political spectrum at the same time? It may be that the political messages were being heard not from the pulpit, but from the pews. In 1988, Wald, Hill, and Owen, a team of political scientists who were interested in the political nature of churches, visited churches from a variety of theological perspectives to observe how political messages can be passed—not just through the message given during the church service but from the entire experience of Sunday worship. What they found was that political views were expressed in every worship space, but often the communication was subtle and subconscious.[40]

In their article, Wald, Hill, and Owen describe their visit to a mainline church where "harvest symbols stressed the need to combat poverty and hunger" and the hymn selection included "folk songs from the civil rights era." In a more conservative evangelical church, the pastor encouraged donations to build a fence around the church property to "protect against beer parties and other rowdy activities taking place nearby." That church had also requested volunteers to help at the local pro-life office. The authors also noted that just by viewing the bumper stickers on the cars in the church parking lot, it was easy to ascertain the political leanings of the congregants of each religious community.[41]

These observations point to an unmistakable fact about American religion and politics: the most consequential time during the Sunday worship service is not when the pastor steps up to the pulpit and begins his sermon. Instead, where the real political messaging occurs is during the few minutes that precede the beginning of formal worship gathering and when people are collecting their things and heading out to the parking lot. During those informal conversations, it's inevitable that politics will crop up as a topic of conversation. Whether an election is drawing near or a national event is dominating the thoughts of the average churchgoer, someone will undoubtedly want to talk to their fellow congregants about what is going on in the world.

However, something else is going on in the average church that I think many people who have never worked in ministry will likely miss. Pastors are disincentivized from being controversial from the pulpit. To understand the precarious position that pastors find themselves in each and every Sunday, we must consider the state of their employment with a local church. Many of the protections afforded to employees in the United States do not necessarily extend to pastors. Churches have almost complete freedom to fire pastors for any reason, at any time, without any legal backlash. Courts have consistently given a wide berth to churches, as they don't want to get involved in theological matters. If relieved of their duties, many pastors are not given a severance package and will lose benefits, such as living in the church's parsonage and participating in a group health insurance plan. Each Sunday a preacher must walk a tightrope.

Consider the position of a pastor when he or she was tasked with writing their Sunday sermon after the death of George Floyd in the summer of 2020. That pastor may have felt theologically compelled to speak about racial injustice and police brutality in the United States. But many pastors were keenly aware of the political positions of their most influential congregants and may have shied away from speaking from the pulpit about such divisive political issues. So instead, they wrote their message using a number of vague statements in hopes of getting their point across without angering anyone in the crowd that morning. A preacher speaking in vagaries about political issues is much more the norm than a pastor boldly declaring that "abortion is murder" or "black lives matter" from the pulpit.

Thus, churches are deeply and inevitably political—but the politics that emerges in the local congregation is typically from the bottom up, not the top down. A random discussion about a tax increase among two business owners before the church service begins is much more likely to occur than a fiery sermon about the sin of homosexuality. A note in the bulletin about a rally to protest income inequality is much more commonplace than a pastor who explicitly endorses a presidential candidate during weekend worship. Churches have always been political, and they will always be political, because groups of people gathered together will always discuss politics. There's no reason to think that will change anytime soon, with or without the Johnson Amendment. There's ample reason to believe that if the Johnson Amendment were repealed, either legislatively or through the courts, not much would change in preachers' sermons each Sunday.

For Further Reading

Djupe, Paul A., and Gilbert, Christopher. *The Prophetic Pulpit: Clergy, Churches, and Communities in American Politics*. Lanham, MD: Rowman & Littlefield, 2003.

This book relies on a tremendous amount of survey data to arrive at the conclusions put forth in this chapter: most pastors go out of their way to be apolitical. What sets this work apart is the authors' analysis of data, not only from churchgoers but clergy as well. Using both datasets allows the authors to explain how there's often a theological and political divide between the pulpit and the pews, with pastors often more liberal than their parishioners.

Goldfeder, Mark A., and Michelle K. Terry. "To Repeal or Not Repeal: The Johnson Amendment." *U. Mem. L. Rev.* 48 (2017): 209.

Goldfeder and Terry explore the history of the Johnson Amendment and the legal implications for the American tax code and the First Amendment's right to freedom of religion. They detail the fact that most churches were steering clear of politics well before the Johnson Amendment became the law of the land.

Wald, Kenneth D., Dennis E. Owen, and Samuel S. Hill. "Churches as Political Communities." *American Political Science Review* 82, no. 2 (1988): 531–48.

This article combines observational results with survey data to help us understand how churches do pass along political messages, whether intentionally or unintentionally. This work also introduces the "self-selection hypothesis" and carefully considers implications of the fact that because people voluntarily associate with a religious community, they can easily leave if they disagree with something about the church.

Conclusion: A Better Path

A FEW WEEKS AGO, I STARTED LOOKING OVER MY notes for my American Foreign Policy course. In the margins of a page focused on the 1960s, I wrote a simple question to myself: "What do we make of Robert McNamara?" In my mind, he's one of the most tragic figures in American foreign policy. McNamara's legacy will always be deeply intertwined with the war in Vietnam. Serving both Presidents Kennedy and Johnson as the Secretary of Defense, McNamara advised them that defeat was not an option in Southeast Asia and that the United States should do whatever it took to stop the spread of communism. Of course, history tells us that McNamara was sorely mistaken, and his approach to the region led to the deaths of tens of thousands of American soldiers, hundreds of thousands of North and South Vietnamese soldiers, and millions of Vietnamese civilians. By 1967, McNamara's resolve had softened, and he told President Johnson that a US victory was not likely in Vietnam. Less than a year later he resigned his position and left US government service entirely.[42]

In his latter years, McNamara became more reflective about his role in the war in Vietnam. In his 1995 memoir, *In Retrospect,* McNamara wrote, "We were wrong, terribly wrong. We owe it to future generations to explain why."[43] A few years later, McNamara's approach to Vietnam was the subject of the award-winning documentary *The Fog of War.* In it, an eighty-five-year-old McNamara speaks quite candidly about the mistakes he made during his tenure as Secretary of Defense. At one point in the interview, he states, "I think the human race needs to think more about killing. How much evil must we do in order to do good?"[44]

It's clear that with the benefit of hindsight and the wisdom that comes with age, McNamara had changed his mind about his actions as a younger man. Unfortunately, those actions led to death and destruction for untold numbers of people both in the United States and Southeast Asia. At least he had the courage to admit that he had made mistakes, however.

A more direct parallel to Robert McNamara was George W. Bush's first Secretary of Defense—Donald Rumsfeld. According to notes taken by a close aide in the hours just after the United States was attacked on September 11th, Rumsfeld was already poised to use the tragedy as a justification for launching a series of military incursions across the globe, whether they were related to the terrorist attacks or not. In the years after his retirement in 2006, there's no evidence that Rumsfeld ever questioned his role in the United States' involvement in conflicts in Iraq and Afghanistan. George Packer, a journalist for the *Atlantic*, wrote upon Rumsfeld's death in June 2021, "His fatal judgment was equaled only by his absolute self-assurance. He lacked the courage to doubt himself. He lacked the wisdom to change his mind."[45]

Both Rumsfeld and McNamara presided over particularly dark moments in American foreign policy. The United States' involvement with Vietnam was, from almost any vantage point, a strategic mistake. In much the same way, the United States' invasion of Afghanistan and Iraq has left us involved in both countries for nearly two decades—costing an incalculable amount of blood and treasure. But I must admit that when I look back over the lives of both McNamara and Rumsfeld, I have immeasurably more respect for the former than I do for the latter. The reason is quite simple: when presented with new information, McNamara changed his mind.

Reevaluating our worldview can be an unnerving experience, because it often leads to a cascade of changes that we cannot anticipate when we begin to think carefully about our perspective on things. But as Socrates famously stated, "The unexamined life is not worth living." The ability for us to reverse course, to think differently about the world, and to approach situations with a set of fresh eyes is what makes this constant introspection all worth it.

My hope in writing this book is that I have given you more than a few reasons to reevaluate your thinking about religion and politics in the United States. You probably believe a lot of things about the social world that are not empirically true. I know I do.

HOW TO HAVE A DIFFICULT CONVERSATION

I believe, however, that a willingness to reflect on information that may change the way we think is always a very good thing. So I want to challenge you to adopt a posture of openness toward new information and to consider as often as possible reevaluating what you believe about the world. I have been trying to do this in my own life the past few years, especially when I am talking to people who have a different view of things than I do. Still, I've had some awkward exchanges recently. As soon as someone asks me what I do for a living, the conversation immediately veers toward religion and politics. Those difficult conversations have led me to think strategically about how I dialogue with other people on topics that can quickly become toxic. Fortunately, after trying out a number of techniques, I think there are ways to facilitate discussion without ending up yelling at each other.

Ask Questions

I often find that my conversation partner is eager to stake out a position on a whole host of topics related to my field of specialization. It used to be the case that when I heard someone state an opinion with which I disagreed, I would immediately express my opposition or challenge them in a confrontational way. People who knew me in high school or college often remarked at how argumentative I was. I was proud of that reputation then. But more recently, I have changed my approach to dialogue. Instead of being directly confrontational, I now respond by asking questions, such as, "Can you help me understand how you arrived at that opinion?" Or, "What am I missing here?"

I've found that asking these questions has a surprising number of benefits. The first is that it automatically lowers the temperature of the debate. As long as questions are posed in a truly inquisitive way, most people are more than willing to continue the conversation. But another benefit of asking questions is that encouraging the other person to state their beliefs aloud helps them work through their own reasoning and perhaps discover the strengths and weaknesses of their mental process. I think we can all admit that there have been times in our lives when we believed something right up to the point when we had to defend our belief to another human being. We quickly realized that we hadn't really thought things through.

Now, I must admit that most of the time when I approach a conversation this way, I come away with the impression that my conversation partner doesn't have a very good grasp of their own rationale. Most people just don't think too deeply about these types of things. I completely understand that. Thinking deeply about religion and politics is, quite literally, my job. I think about them entirely too much. But that doesn't mean I have seen all the angles and considered all the possibilities. At times, someone I am speaking with will raise a point I had never considered before. When they do that, they are giving me an incredible gift. But I must be willing to receive that gift with openness and gratitude, which is not always easy.

Stop Arguing about Things on Social Media

However, I have to state plainly—if you are arguing about politics, religion, or anything of any importance at all on social media, I am almost certain that you are wasting your time, as well as the time of your discussion partner. While academic research on social media is incredibly new and we are still trying to theorize just how social media changes our understanding of human communication—there's ample evidence that it's a poor substitute for in-person dialogue.

In just the past few years, a consensus has emerged that the algorithms that power the most popular social media platforms are designed to "exploit the human brain's attraction to divisiveness."[46] Social media algorithms are constructed and refined in pursuit of increased user engagement, and conflict is the easiest way to attract eyeballs, drive clicks, and draw new user signups. The type of engagement that occurs on those platforms is of secondary concern; the primary goal is increasing profit margin.

In a study of 4.7 million posts on Twitter and Facebook, a research team investigated a central question of the social media age: what makes content go viral? What these scholars found was obvious but disheartening—posts that labeled an opponent as a member of an out-group were much more likely to get shared than those that did not. Specifically, when a politician running for office described their opponent with political terms like "liberal" or "conservative," they increased the chances that their message would reach a wider audience. One of the members of the research team, Steve Rathje, a doctoral student in psychology at the University of Cambridge, told a reporter from NBC, "We think this cycle, these incentives for virality, are essentially creating a toxic ecosystem."[47]

Think about what happens as soon as you see a fight brewing in the comments on a controversial topic. If you are anything like me, you feel compelled to start scrolling through the comments and looking for the conflict to escalate. Most of the commenters are not truly trying to engage with another person on the internet. They are actually playing to the crowd, all of us who continue to scroll through and hit the "thumbs up" reaction emojis at the bottom of each post. These debates are performative and nothing else. How often have you seen anything like a Facebook debate happen in a face-to-face setting? I'm going to guess not very often. If you are truly seeking to have an honest and open conversation with another human being, please don't do so on social media.

Recognize You Might Be Wrong

I will never forget a story I read in *Flickering Pixels: How Technology Shapes Your Faith* by Shane Hipps. He recounts an event in his Mennonite church. One of the older men, Paul, stood up to reflect on his life during morning worship. Paul was supposed to be drafted to fight the Nazis in World War II, but because a central tenet of his faith was nonviolence, he sought out an exemption from the fighting as a conscientious objector. He was ostracized by his community for taking this position and was made to serve in a hospital for the severely mentally ill.

While in this facility he was charged with taking care of patients who were incredibly violent and were often restrained in straitjackets and solitary confinement. Paul and a number of other Mennonite men were placed in these facilities as punishment for their unwillingness to take up arms against the evil of the Third Reich. But those men took their assignment as an opportunity to help those patients in their care. They resolved that no matter how much they were physically or verbally abused, they would not respond in kind to those who were suffering. Instead, they developed an approach to therapy called "gentle teaching," the goal of which is to not focus on a person's behavior but instead the cause of that behavior as a way to reduce judgment and shame. This approach is still used in mental hospitals today.

Paul told that story to his congregation on that Sunday. Everyone in the crowd felt the weight of all that he had given up based on his beliefs. He had suffered broken bones and social isolation. He noted that he responded to violence with gentleness because that's what he thought Jesus would do. But before Paul sat down, he said something that is worth remembering: "But ...I could be wrong."[48]

That's a posture we just don't see a lot in modern American discourse. Everyone seems to have an opinion. Whether based on decades of study or reading the headlines of a few news articles, we all want to stake out a position. But maybe we shouldn't. Maybe we should be a bit more humble, like Paul. When someone asks what we think and how we feel about something, we should often be inclined to state, "I don't know enough about that topic to have an opinion." In the twenty-first century, we can be too smart, too rich, or too arrogant, but it's very hard to be too humble.

I hope this book has humbled you a bit and helped you reconsider how you think about the social world around us. I can tell you that it has certainly humbled me. There were at least a dozen myths I wanted to include in these pages, but once I actually wrote them out, I realized I was wrong about them myself. Thus, I hope we have learned together. May we never stop learning, growing, being challenged, and changing our minds. It's a difficult road, but aren't the most treacherous paths often the best ones?

Appendix: Data Sources

COOPERATIVE ELECTION STUDY (CES)

While the first wave was conducted in 2006, the survey didn't really find its footing until 2008 and has only been getting larger and more reliable since then. It has been conducted every year since 2008 and has become a tremendous resource for scholars of American political and religious life. One of the reasons is the sheer size of the sample. In 2016, there were 64,600 respondents and in 2020 there were 61,000. The years in which there is not a major election typically have a smaller sample (the survey conducted in 2019 had 18,000 respondents), but this is still incredibly large compared to other surveys in the social sciences.

The study has always been conducted in an online format, which means respondents read and respond to the questions on their computer, tablet, or phone. The sampling population is all adults, 18 years and older, living in the United States. The respondents are recruited by a survey firm called YouGov, which has a strong reputation in the world of polling. Those participating in the CES are compensated for their time. The *Economist* contracts with YouGov to do their surveys as well.

The CES uses the same basic framework for religion questions that was pioneered by the team at the Pew Research Center, which means that the results from a CES survey are directly comparable to other statistics put out in Pew reports on religion. The results that are relayed here are always calculated with the appropriate survey weights supplied by the team at the Cooperative Election Study, which is based out of Harvard University.

In addition to the longitudinal surveys mentioned above, the CES team also conducted a panel survey from 2010 through 2014, which was crucial data when trying to track how people changed their behavior after becoming born-again.

The data from the CES is available to download for free from their website: https://cces.gov.harvard.edu/.

GENERAL SOCIAL SURVEY (GSS)

The General Social Survey may be the most important survey instrument in the history of academic social science in the United States. Begun in 1972 by a team of scholars based out of the National Opinion Research Center, it has been conducted at least biannually since its inception. Many of the questions in the GSS have been asked using the same wording and offering the same response options for the last forty-six years. Thus, it provides the most accurate instrument to gauge the social, political, and religious changes happening in the United States over time.

The General Social Survey has always been conducted in a face-to-face format during the entirety of existence. However, that changed in 2020 due to restrictions surrounding the COVID-19 pandemic, forcing the GSS to move to an online format. This has led to a significant delay in the release of the 2020 data which is why it is not included in this book.

One significant disadvantage to the General Social Survey when comparing it to the Cooperative Election Study is sample size. The average GSS wave is just about 2,200 respondents. That makes studying smaller religious groups very difficult using the GSS. All results reported in this book include the proper weight supplied by the team at the GSS.

The General Social Survey has a tremendous website with an online version of their codebook that is very easy to navigate. Alongside free raw data downloads, the team at the NORC also offers tools that allow the general public to do some basic data analysis of the GSS data in their web browser. All of this can be accessed through their website: http://gss.norc.org/.

PROPRIETARY SURVEYS

In two myths for this book, I relied on data that was collected through surveys that are not publicly available. In the myth focused on support for female clergy, a team of researchers including myself and Paul Djupe (Denison University) managed to secure funds to conduct a survey in Fall 2019. The total sample size was 3,136 respondents. We used Qualtrics, a leading survey firm to recruit and conduct our survey. That data is not currently available for download to the general public, but our hope is to make it publicly available in the near future.

The other proprietary survey that was used in this book is in the myth about the amount of political discussion that occurs from the pulpit. The data for that effort comes from a survey that was also conducted using Qualtrics. However, the funding for that effort came from a research grant that Paul Djupe and I secured through the Louisville Institute. We applied through their Project Grants for Researchers and the title of our proposal was, "The Social and Political Implications of Non-Denominational Protestantism." Our survey consisted of five hundred denominational Protestants and five hundred nondenominational Protestants. In addition to the results displayed in this book, Paul and I have begun to write up the findings from that project into a book-length treatment. Our hope is to publish that book (along with the data) in the near future.

VOTER STUDY GROUP

The Democracy Fund, a nonpartisan and independent foundation, is an organization focused on identifying challenges and threats to democracy. To that end, they have funded the Voter Study Group, which is based out of UCLA. The Voter Study Group has conducted a number of surveys that assess the political behaviors and beliefs of Americans. Two of their surveys were used in this volume.

The VOTER (Views of the Electorate Research Survey) data is a panel design where the same sets of respondents were contacted every few years from 2012 to 2019. They were asked many of the same questions, allowing researchers to track changes over time at the individual level. There were over 2,000 respondents who answered each wave of the survey.

The Nationscape survey is another data collection effort that is unrivaled in its size. Each week from July 2019 through December 2020, they surveyed over 3,000 Americans using the survey firm Lucid. While the last segment of data has not been released, the first twelve months of responses were analyzed for this book. The total sample size was over 300,000 respondents.

Notes

1 Pew Research Center, "1. Public Views on Climate Change and Climate Scientists," October 4, 2016, https://www.pewresearch.org/science/2016/10/04/public-views-on-climate-change-and-climate-scientists/.

2 R. J. Reinhart, "Few in U.S. Continue to See Vaccines as Important," Gallup, January 14, 2020, https://news.gallup.com/poll/276929/fewer-continue-vaccines-important.aspx.

3 Lisa Lerer, "Giuliani in Public: 'It's a Fraud.' Giuliani in Court: 'This Is Not a Case,'" *New York Times*, Nov. 18, 2020, https://www.nytimes.com/2020/11/18/us/politics/trump-giuliani-voter-fraud.html.

4 Bacon Jr., Perry. "Democrats Are Wrong About Republicans. Republicans Are Wrong About Democrats." FiveThirtyEight. June 26, 2018. https://fivethirtyeight.com/features/democrats-are-wrong-about-republicans-republicans-are-wrong-about-democrats/.

5 James Baldwin, "As Much Truth As One Can Bear," in *The Cross of Redemption: Uncollected Writings*, ed. Randall Kenan (New York, NY: Vintage, 2011), 33.

6 Lily Rothman, "Is God Dead? At 50," *Time*, April 7, 2016, https://time.com/isgoddead/.

7 Derek Thompson. "Three Decades Ago, America Lost Its Religion. Why?" *Atlantic*. 2019. https://www.theatlantic.com/ideas/archive/2019/09/atheism-fastest-growing-religion-us/598843/. Accessed September 3, 2021.

8 Bonnie Kristian. "The Coming End of Christian America." 2019. *Week*. https://theweek.com/articles/872709/coming-end-christian-america. Accessed: September 3, 2021.

9 Burge, Ryan P. 2021. *The Nones: Where They Came From, Who They Are, and Where They Are Going*. Minneapolis, MN: Fortress Press, 2021.

10 Jones, Robert P., 2016. *The End of White Christian America*. Simon and Schuster: New York, NY.

11 Pew Research Center. "In U.S., Decline of Christianity Continues at a Rapid Pace." 2019. https://www.pewforum.org/2019/10/17/in-u-s-decline-of-christianity-continues-at-rapid-pace/. Accessed September 3, 2021.

12 Peter Wehner. "The Deepening Crisis in Evangelical Christianity." 2019. *Atlantic*. https://www.theatlantic.com/ideas/archive/2019/07/evangelical-christians-face-deepening-crisis/593353/. Accessed September 3, 2021.

13 R. Laurence Moore and Isaac Kramnick. "Blame Evangelicals for the Decline in Christian Faith." 2018. *Daily Beast.*https://www.thedailybeast.com/blame-evangelicals-for-the-decline-in-christian-faith. Accessed: September 3, 2021.

14 Jennifer Agiesta. "Poll: Donald Trump Surges to 32% Support." *CNN*. https://www.cnn.com/2015/09/10/politics/donald-trump-ben-carson-cnn-poll/index.html. Accessed: September 3, 2021.

15 Tim Carney. *Alienated America: Why Some Places Thrive While Others Collapse.* 2019. HarperCollins: New York, NY.

16 Public Religion Research Institute. "Dueling Realities: Amid Multiple Crises, Trump and Biden Supporters See Different Priorities and Futures for the Nation." 2020. https://www.prri.org/research/amid-multiple-crises-trump-and-biden-supporters-see-different-realities-and-futures-for-the-nation/. Accessed: September 3, 2021.

17 Tricia C. Bruce, *How Americans Understand Abortion: A Comprehensive Interview Study of Abortion Attitudes in the U.S.* (South Bend, IN: University of Notre Dame, McGrath Institute for Church Life, 2020), 53, https://news.nd.edu/assets/395804/how_americans_understand_abortion_final_7_15_20.pdf, accessed May 17, 2021.

18 Ruth Benedict. *The Chrysanthemum and the Sword.* 1946. Houghton Mifflin: Boston, MA.

19 Stephanie McCrummen, Beth Reinhard, and Alice Crites. "Woman says Roy Moore initiated sexual encounter when she was 14, he was 32." *Washington Post.* November 9, 2017. https://www.washingtonpost.com/investigations/woman-says-roy-moore-initiated-sexual-encounter-when-she-was-14-he-was-32/2017/11/09/1f495878-c293-11e7-afe9-4f60b5a6c4a0_story.html. Accessed: September 4, 2021.

20 Jenny Jarvie. "For Republicans in upscale Alabama suburbs, Roy Moore presents a conundrum." *Los Angeles Times*. November 17, 2017. https://www.latimes.com/politics/la-na-alabama-moore-suburbs-20171117-story.html. Accessed: September 4, 2021.

21 Jenny Jarvie. "For Republicans in upscale Alabama suburbs, Roy Moore presents a conundrum." *Los Angeles Times*. November 17, 2017. https://www.latimes.com/politics/la-na-alabama-moore-suburbs-20171117-story.html. Accessed: September 4, 2021.

22 Resolution On Abortion And Sanctity Of Human Life. 1974 Annual Meeting of the Southern Baptist Convention. https://www.sbc.net/resource-library/resolutions/resolution-on-abortion-and-sanctity-of-human-life/. Accessed: September 4, 2021.

23 Resolution On Abortion And Sanctity Of Human Life. 1976 Annual Meeting of the Southern Baptist Convention. https://www.sbc.net/resource-library/resolutions/resolution-on-abortion-and-sanctity-of-human-life/. Accessed: September 4, 2021.

24 Balmer, Randall. *Thy Kingdom Come: How the Religious Right Distorts Faith and Threatens America.* 2006. Basic Books: New York, NY.

25 Frank, Thomas. 2004. *What's the Matter with Kansas? How Conservatives Won the Heart of America.* 2004. Metropolitan Books: New York, NY.

26 Thomas Roberts and Sean Gibbons. "Same-sex marriage bans winning on state ballots." *CNN.* November 3, 2004. https://www.cnn.com/2004/ALLPOLITICS/11/02/ballot.samesex.marriage/. Accessed: September 4, 2021.

27 Theodore Schleifer, "Why Some Conservatives Are Upset with Ted Cruz on Immigration," *CNN*, Nov. 12, 2015, https://www.cnn.com/2015/11/12/politics/ted-cruz-immigration-h1-b-visas.

28 Jill Lawrence. "Bush Administration Getting Tired of Buchanan's Symbolic Victories." Associated Press. March 4, 1992. https://apnews.com/article/e205d6b4297e2b6639a90c3b5e504afb. Accessed: September 4, 2021.

29 Patrick Joseph Buchanan, "Culture War Speech: Address to the Republican National Convention (August 17, 1992)," *Voices of Democracy: The U.S. Oratory Project*, https://voicesofdemocracy.umd.edu/buchanan-culture-war-speech-speech-text/, accessed May 17, 2021.

30 This is discussed in more depth in Myth 11.

31 The Baptist Faith and Message – Section 6: The Church. https://bfm.sbc.net/bfm2000/#vi-the-church. Accessed: September 4, 2021.

32 Robert McClory, "Pope Francis and Women's Ordination," *National Catholic Reporter*, September 16, 2013, https://www.ncronline.org/blogs/francis-chronicles/pope-francis-and-womens-ordination.

33 Hopkins, A.G. "American Empire: A Global History." 2018. Page 301. Princeton University Press: Princeton, NJ.

34 Burge, Ryan. *The Nones: Where They Came From, Who They Are, and Where They Are Going*. Chapter 1. Fortress Press: Minneapolis, MN.

35 Deborah Jian Lee. "Why the Young Religious Right Is Leaning Left," *Time*, 2015, https://time.com/4078909/evangelical-millennials.

36 Eliza Griswold, "Millennial Evangelicals Diverge from Their Parents' Beliefs," *New Yorker*, 2018,

https://www.newyorker.com/news/on-religion/millennial-evangelicals-diverge-from-their-parents-beliefs.

37 Due to issues with survey sample size, it's not possible to assess the voting patterns of young evangelicals prior to 2008.

38 National Council of Nonprofits. Fact Sheet on Johnson Amendment: Trump Foundation Litigation and Pending Legislation. https://www.councilofnonprofits.org/fact-sheet-johnson-amendment-trump-foundation-litigation-and-pending-legislation. Accessed: September 4, 2021.

39 Scott, Eugene. "At a National Day of Prayer speech, Trump falsely claims there was little religious freedom before his election." *Washington Post*. May 2, 2019. https://www.washingtonpost.com/politics/2019/05/02/national-day-prayer-speech-trump-falsely-claims-there-was-little-religious-freedom-before-his-election/. Accessed: September 4, 2021.

40 Wald, Kenneth D., Dennis E. Owen, and Samuel S. Hill. "Churches as Political Communities." *The American Political Science Review* 82, no. 2 (1988): 531–48. Accessed September 4, 2021. doi:10.2307/1957399.

41 All quotes in this paragraph were taken from page 533.

42 Eschner, Kat. "How Robert McNamara Came to Regret the War He Escalated." *Smithsonian*. November 29, 2016. https://www.smithsonianmag.com/smart-news/why-robert-mcnamara-came-regret-war-he-escalated-180961231/. Accessed: September 4, 2021.

43 Robert McNamara, *In Retrospect: The Tragedy and Lessons of Vietnam* (Vintage, 1995), XVII.

44 Errol Morris and Robert S. McNamara, *The Fog of War* (Sony Pictures Home Entertainment, 2005).

45 George Packer, "How Rumsfeld Deserves to Be Remembered," *Atlantic*, June 30, 2021, https://www.theatlantic.com/ideas/archive/2021/06/how-donald-rumsfeld-deserves-be-remembered/619334/.

46 Jeff Horwitz and Deep Seetharaman. "Facebook Executives Shut Down Efforts to Make the Site Less Divisive." *Wall Street Journal*. May 26, 2020. https://www.wsj.com/articles/facebook-knows-it-encourages-division-top-executives-nixed-solutions-11590507499. Accessed: September 4, 2021.

47 David Ingram, "How to Go Viral on Social Media? Attack a Political Opponent, Study Says," *NBC News*, 2021. https://www.nbcnews.com/tech/tech-news/go-viral-social-media-attack-political-opponent-study-says-rcna1277. Accessed July 3, 2021.

48 Shane Shane Hipps, *Flickering Pixels: How Technology Shapes Your Faith* (New York: Harper Collins, 2019), 157–159.